THE
Paranoid's
Hanbdook

CHRISTOPHER HYDE

KEY PORTER·BOOKS

To
Richard M. Nixon, the Father of Modern Paranoia

and to
Alfred E. Newman, "What, me worry?"

The publisher greatfully acknowledges the assistance of the Canada Council and the Ontario Arts Council.

CANADIAN CATALOGUING IN PUBLICATION DATA

Hyde, Christopher, 1949–
Paranoid's handbook

ISBN 1-55013-463-9

I. Title

PS8565.Y34P37 1993   C818'.5402   C93-094226-4
PR9199.3.H94P37 1993

Key Porter Books Limited
70 The Esplanade
Toronto, ON
M5E 1R2

Design: Scott Richardson
Printed and bound in Canada

93 94 95 96 5 4 3 2 1

Contents

Introduction

T*he Encyclopedia of Human Behavior* (Doubleday, 1970, Vol. 2) defines paranoia as: "A psychotic disorder marked by slowly developing, systemized delusions of persecution. . . . often a gross exaggeration of tendencies found among normal individuals."

By the 1985 edition of the *Diagnostic and Statistical Manual of Mental Disorders*, the American Psychiatric Association (APA) was hedging its bets: ". . . generalized suspicion, letter writing, complaints about social injustices and instigation of legal action are frequent. . . . the conjugal paranoiac may become convinced that his or her mate has been unfaithful."

By 1992 the APA had concluded that there was no such mental disorder as paranoia, and the diagnostics and definitions were removed from their casebooks, except for such extreme examples as hallucinations of giant insect swarms coming through time portals in the Van Allen Radiation Belt caused by freon from old refrigerators.

It is interesting to note that during this period – 1970-1992 – the United States elected at least three presidents who would have fallen under earlier definitions of paranoia: "You won't have me to kick around any more" Nixon, "Evil Empire" Reagan and "The Media-Hollywood Link" Bush.

It was also discovered during this time that the so-called conjugal paranoid had probably been right all along. A lot of married people *were* out there screwing around like crazy (69.1 percent of married women over 35, and 84.4 percent of married men).

If you went to see a psychiatrist about your own or your husband's philandering you stood a decent chance of being sexually molested by your shrink. (In a recent survey 10 percent of U.S. psychiatrists admitted to having sex with at least one of their patients.)

Fifty years ago an evening stroll across New York's Central Park was the stuff of pocket-book romance; now it is an act of madness. In the vanished Norman Rockwell world, the dog was man's best friend; now he deposits 10,000 tons of doggie-doo on North America's lawns every day, spreading a pestilential plague of toxoplasmosis, visceral larva migrans, and leptospirosis. Long-dormant volcanoes like Mt. Saint Helens are blowing their tops with increasing frequency, earthquakes are levelling our cities one by one, and the life expectancy of an 18-year-old in East L.A. is shorter than that of a child in Bangladesh. We know of 50 times more serial killers on the loose right now than were reported in the last 100 years, a war breaks out somewhere every six days, and there is enough radioactive waste stored in Rhode Island alone to wipe out the world 10 times over. And the red pimento in stuffed olives is really colored cellulose.

The world, it seems, has changed and the paranoid, once scoffed at, has come into his own. So for all of you out there who know in your hearts that somebody or something is lurking, ready to do you wrong when you least expect it, read on.

Unless, that is, you're too paranoid.

The Fear of...

FLYING

(Jong's Syndrome)

THE PARANOID CERTAINTY:
"Deregulation, bankruptcies, Ronald Reagan and metal fatigue make every flight I take like a ride on the Titanic.*"*

THE FACILE REASSURANCE:
"Technology has advanced so far in the last few years that flying is safer than going to the bathroom in your own home."

THE OBJECTIVE TRUTH:

Whoever said going to the bathroom in your own home was safe? In 1990 there were 9 million accidents causing permanent disability in the United States – 3.2 million of which took place in the home; 21,000 of them were fatal. Most were of the "I've fallen and I can't get up" variety (14,800); half occurred in the bathroom. Firearms accounted for 65,000 accidents and 1,140 deaths, while another 3,400 choked to death in the kitchen and 1,820 people poisoned themselves. This doesn't include 23,440 homicides, some of which presumably took place in the john.

The people who put together statistics about airplane disasters are an odd bunch who use some pretty far-fetched parameters to come up with their "friendly skies" figures. Take "passenger miles flown".

The statisticians first total the number of passenger miles flown each year – roughly one billion; then they divide in the number of deaths. You, the passenger, usually come up an odds-on favorite. What they neglect to include in the calculations is the fact that the pilot and co-pilot of each airplane are passengers too, not to mention the stewardesses and stewards.

To get a real figure you have to count up the total number of miles flown by each and every airplane, and *then* divide in the death rate. When you do, things look a little bleak.

> Statistically, there will be 57 airline disasters around the world next year. Your chances of surviving one are virtually nil.

Any professional gambler will tell you that predictions about aircraft disasters involve so many factors that real odds-making is almost impossible. Nonsense. The reality is simple: of every 100,000 people who board an airplane next year, 11 will die. That doesn't seem to be great cause for concern, but those deaths aren't spread evenly throughout the travelling population. Statistically, there will be 57 airline disasters around the world next year; your chances of surviving one are virtually nil.

You can hedge your bets, however. Since 1974 there have been 25 fatal accidents involving aircraft manufactured by Boeing, 16 involving aircraft manufactured by McDonnell Douglas, and only two involving British Aerospace equipment. Warsaw, the Canary Islands, and Spain are statistically poor choices as destinations; Thailand is to be avoided at all costs. As most accidents take place during take-off and landing, O'Hare Airport in Chicago is potentially the most dangerous, with Heathrow running a very close second.

Mexico City Airport is an accident waiting to happen, as pilots pay no attention to the air-traffic controllers and simply aim their aircraft in the direction they want to go. As for terrorists, Athens Airport and Tokyo are the terminals of choice for the few loonie groups still in business in these post-Glasnost days.

A lot of people are afraid of flying but eventually become numbed to the horrifying realities of being suspended 38,000 feet up in an air-conditioned cigar tube. They should remember that a Boeing 747 has 1,483,260 parts, any one of which might have been made on a Monday.

FAST FOOD

(Ronald's Revenge)

THE PARANOID CERTAINTY:
"Billions served, but billions of what?"

THE FACILE REASSURANCE:
"It's cheap, it tastes good, and the kids love it."

THE OBJECTIVE TRUTH:

F ast food is everywhere. It lurks on prime corners where banks used to be. It waits, grinning evilly, next to high schools. It hustles in Red Square. And Trafalgar Square. And Times Square. Even Tiananmen Square.

When a fast-food company tells you that its burgers are made from 100 percent beef, they aren't kidding: hooves, horns, tails – even eyeballs. The lettuce they slap on top has: (a) been soaked in a soup of nitrates and sodas to keep it looking green, and (b) probably been fast-frozen for as long as two years. You didn't think those tomatoes were born that red, did you?

Until forced to by law, virtually none of the fast-food producers put an ounce of dairy product into their "shakes", which is why they weren't called "milk" shakes. "Petroleum by-product oil-based floats" wouldn't have gained market share. Nor would the knowledge that the thickener they still use for shakes is the same stuff they use in porn films to portray various body fluids. (In one recent soft-core sci-fi spoof four ounces of fast-food "shake" thickener combined with 200 gallons of Cream of Wheat for a somewhat startling special effect.)

If you're lucky, the flecky bits of green in the relish are pickle pieces rather than dyed wood chips. The fries are heavily salted so you'll buy lots of soda pop, sugar is sprinkled on the buns to make them brown, and don't even think about the slightly chewy parts in the "chicken" sandwich. "Hey, Mom! They're having a special on McBeak Burgers!"

I once asked the president of a huge fast-food chain why the company colors were brown and gold. "Brown for the shit we serve them and gold for the money they pay," she answered with a smile. I also spoke to a

> If you're lucky, the flecky bits of green in the relish are pickle pieces rather than dyed wood chips.

meat-plant worker, whose job was to sit by the rendering tank and plink at the rats running across the stirring paddles. The rendering tanks provide the "oil" for deep-frying. Presumably the rats that were boiled along with everything else added that soupçon of exotic flavor. Or maybe it came from the fact that the rendering tank was also used as a urinal.

Good taste prevents me from describing what happens to the cherries and apples in the fruit pies. Just say no.

THE OBJECTIVE TRUTH:

They've got your number. Driver's license number, social security number, voter registration number, birth registration number, telephone number, credit card number. Your "number" may be on file with as many as 50 government and private agencies, monitored and maintained by hundreds of thousands of people with nothing better to do than make your life miserable by burying you under a mountain of useless paperwork. If you live in the United States, Canada, or the United Kingdom, you appear on about 850 data banks.

There is definitely more going on than bureaucratic make-work. In the United States the National Security Agency taps into every trans atlantic or trans pacific telephone call. The NSA computers, which do the listening, are keyed to respond to specific "trigger" words in conversations. The tapes begin to roll when you use words such as "communist", "drugs", or even "terminate". Depending on the paranoia level of the people programming the computers you might even get into trouble for using the word "coke". This same system is also used by Britain's GCHQ and France's DS9.

You may not be a major drug lord or a seditious spy, but someone out there is on your case. One late payment on a loan, or a credit card pur-

(Orwell's Chorea)

chase returned because the goods were defective can get you into hot water with the Credit Bureau. Even after you've paid the debt, the black mark stays on your file. Forever.

Most large bureaucracies have their own "intelligence gathering" divisions. Revenue Canada, the Internal Revenue Service in the United States and Inland Revenue in the United Kingdom employ battalions of accounting spies to develop files that often include sexual inclinations and drinking habits. Moreover, they cheerfully give out such information without your permission.

Even if you lead a lily-white existence and never make overseas telephone calls you're still under surveillance by Big Brother. Most major telephone companies in North America and Europe employ "quality" checkers who randomly listen in on conversations, supposedly to check the quality of service. What they're really doing is circumventing the wiretap laws. These companies have carte blanche to do their random listening, unlike the police who have to get a court order. So the agency, police or what-have-you has the company "randomly" listen in on a number they're interested in, without the bother of due process. In the United States approximately 10,000 of these "random" numbers are under surveillance each day.

Even if you're not a large government agency or police organization, phone tapping is relatively easy. Criminal Research Products Inc. in the Unite States offers a simple gizmo for $595. It sucks up any telephone conversation in a 300-yard radius and sends it to any phone you choose. Cal-Tronix sells a slightly less sophisticated version for $29.95. So, if you can't lick 'em, join 'em. Your only alternative is to parachute onto a desert island and play Robinson Crusoe.

OTHER "

TAKING A VACATION
(Lost Luggage Palsy)

THE PARANOID CERTAINTY:
"Because I look like a tourist I'm going to get ripped off/mugged/raped/murdered."

THE FACILE REASSURANCE:
"You've just seen 30 seconds of Club Med, can you imagine two weeks?"

THE OBJECTIVE TRUTH:

O nce upon a time you looked forward to your vacation. You dreamed about those two weeks in Europe, the safari in Africa or the winter escape to the Caribbean.

Forget it. Travelling is getting more dangerous by the minute (see: Flying). Even if you get there safely it's more than likely that something awful is going to happen to you.

Take Canada, for instance. A nice, peaceful country, right? Sparkling lakes, majestic mountains, Mounties in scarlet uniforms, smiling Inuit and happy-go-lucky Québécois ready to feed you maple syrup or make you a cute shrunken-apple doll.

Not so. Canada is a seething hell-hole of crime and degradation. Each year 15 million tourists invade the land of the beaver and the maple leaf, and each year 1,650,000 of them are victims of criminal activity. Canada is one of the top five countries for being raped, having your car stolen or being involved in a fraudulent or counterfeit-currency transaction. Canada is number four world-wide in criminal offenses.

So, where is it safe? Avoid all Caribbean countries. The Bahamas has the largest per-capita number of violent crimes against tourists, closely followed by St. Kitts, Nevis, Jamaica, and Trinidad. These are also the places where you are most likely to be raped and have your car stolen (except for Switzerland, which has the highest world-wide rate of auto theft). Jamaica and the Bahamas are also among the top five places where the hole in the ozone is biggest, which means you are more likely to develop skin cancer after your week on the beach. The Bahamas also holds the record for the most fish-bone choking deaths, so stay away from the catch of the day.

> The Bahamas has the largest per-capita number of violent crimes against tourists. It also holds the record for the most fish-bone choking deaths.

Medical paranoids should avoid the world's "G" spots – Guinea-Bissau, Guinea and Gambia have the world's highest death rates, lowest number of physicians and least access to health care facilities. The "U" countries – United States, Uganda and the United Kingdom – have the highest incidence of AIDS. On a positive note, it is unlikely that you will be attacked, raped or otherwise inconvenienced in Ethiopia, which has a 0.2 overall crime rate.

Malta is probably your best bet as a tourist destination, and Burkina Faso undoubtedly the worst. On the other hand, getting to Malta involves several highly suspect airport facilities, and no one in his right mind would go to Burkina Faso in the first place. There's nothing to do, nothing to see, nowhere to go and nothing to spend your money on. There are no mountains to climb, rivers to swim in, lakes to sail on or beaches to fry on. The only value in going to Burkina Faso is the cachet of having the stamp in your passport. For the curious among you, in Burkina Faso, that small, arid blot in northwestern Africa surrounded by Mali, the Ivory Coast, Ghana and Niger, life expectancy is 51.6 years, which is a long time to do nothing.

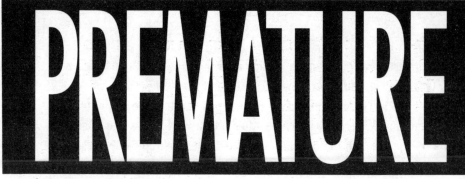

PREMATURE

(Minuteman Syndrome)

THE PARANOID CERTAINTY:
"If she blinks twice she'll miss it."

THE FACILE REASSSURANCE:
*"It's the bottom of the ninth inning,
Smith is on first . . ."*

THE OBJECTIVE TRUTH:

T**HE MOST COMMON OBSTACLE TO WOMEN'S ENJOYMENT** of sexual intercourse, according to women, is the **MAN'S INABILITY** to delay his orgasm. An American study has concluded that 75 percent of men **EJACULATE WITHIN TWO MINUTES** of insertion. This is what Winston Churchill would have called a **CONUNDRUM**: he **CAN'T** so she doesn't. Women barely have time to get used to the idea before the idea is yesterday's news.

There are lots of reasons for PE, from fear that the kids are about to hammer on the door to that exotic paranoia in its own right, the infamous "Vagina Dentata". Uncircumcised men are prone to being **HAIR-TRIG-GERED**, so we may have more PE to look forward to as circumcision has been deemed politically incorrect by most New Age Woo-Woo doctors.

Foreskins aside for the moment, your **PE PROBLEMS** may be education-induced. Of those seeking help for ejaculatory problems, 95 percent were middle- and upper-middle-income earners; less than 1 percent were grade-school or high-school drop-outs.

Most PE is caused by early conditioning. If you spent a lot of time trying to sow your wild oats in her parents' rumpus room or the back seat

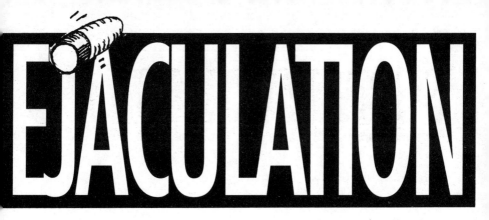

EJACULATION

of the old man's Rambler you might have been setting yourself up for a fall. In middle age it's usually caused by the time-and-motion paradigm: the man who is bored with his partner simply wants to **GET IT OVER WITH** so he can get to sleep.

Some of the classic cures for PE include the old **BASEBALL STATS** trick, penguins and icicles, or thinking about that looming balloon payment on the mortgage. So much for sex as fun. Masters and Johnson claim a 90 percent success rate with their "squeeze" technique to **INHIBIT** ejaculation: the woman **GRASPS** the appropriate organ at the base, **JAMS** her thumb into the flesh just above the testicles, and **CRUSHES** the upper end of the organ with her hand. M & J don't recommend **VICE-GRIPS**. You can see why the technique works, but you're left with the possibility of reversing the problem and **NEVER COMING AGAIN**.

You can also try a variety of **ANESTHETICS**, available from the back pages of some magazines or the shelves of your local drugstore. These would seem to **DEFEAT** the purpose of the event and might also reverse the problem, causing **RETARDED EJACULATION**, in which you go on forever. This may seem like God's gift to women, but don't kid yourself. Ninety minutes of non-stop intercourse leads only to **FRUSTRATION** and **FRICTION**.

The **REALLY NASTY THING** about PE is that **THE WORSE IT GETS, THE WORSE IT GETS**. Monasteries and income tax offices are full of men who found themselves **TRAPPED** on that merry-go-round. Even Masters and Johnson will tell you that the only cure for Premature Ejaculation is to forget about it and stop worrying. Mind you, that happy couple of gurus is no longer together so maybe we'll have to think this whole thing through again. Novocain? Scaffolding? **RUBBER BANDS?**

SUPERMARKETS

("Attention Shoppers" Syndrome)

THE PARANOID CERTAINTY:
"Barcodes were invented by a Satanic cult of cost accountants."

THE FACILE REASSURANCE:
"Supermarkets save time and money, and the parking is free."

THE OBJECTIVE TRUTH:

Supermarkets are the twilight zone of the food industry. There are more tricks, scams and low blows dealt in those aisles than in a lawyer's office. Your average Safeway or Piggly-Wiggly operates on a profit margin of 1 to 3 percent; this means they have to buy in enormous volume, and so do you. They get you in the mood as soon as you go through the automatic doors. The music you hear is specially composed, recorded and programmed to sneak into your wallet. It's like Little Bo-Peep leading her lambs to the abattoir: if you're listening to Mantovani or the "Blue Danube", how can you be led astray?

Easily.

Nothing in a supermarket is what it seems to be. Take "hollow-blocking": a large delivery of frozen goods will arrive at a store, looking scrumptious. On the outside. Inside the block of food is the bruised, grey or otherwise nasty stuff that the wholesaler couldn't get rid of. The farmer does it to the shipper, the shipper does it to the freezer company, the freezer company does it to the wholesaler, and so on down the line, till the supermarket does it to you. The tray of tasty-looking tomatoes usually has squished and/or slightly rotten ones packed on the bottom; the box of strawberries has the moldy ones in the middle; and the tiny, wizened chicken breast is hidden where you can't see it until it's too late.

Meat, of course, is where the supermarket truly shines. What's the difference between "regular" and "lean" ground beef? The fat content you say?

Uh-uh. Regular is ordinary ground beef put through the mincer once; lean is put through the mincer twice. How many times does "extra lean" go through? You guessed it.

It takes the average supermarket butcher less than six seconds to cut up a chicken, yet the price difference between the whole thing and the separate pieces can be as much as 25 percent per pound. Sometimes they don't do anything, and boost the price anyway. A supermarket in New York charges one price for Porterhouse steak and another for T-Bone, even though they are exactly the same cut. "Aged" or "marbled" beef usually means it was left in the truck with the freezer off. The next time you're at the meat counter, look up – check out the light fixtures. You'll notice that they use photographer's tungsten lamps to add a little blue to the visible spectrum. This enhances the reds and pinks in the meat below.

Let's move on to the produce department. Got a shipment of second-rate green beans? Take a box of top-quality beans and sprinkle lightly over the display. Why does lettuce come in those nasty plastic wrappers? To keep the outer leaves closed so you can't see the discolored ones underneath. Want to make green bananas yellow really fast – put them into the cyanide chamber overnight. If anyone asks, tell him you do it to make sure any immigrant tarantulas get snuffed before they crawl out from under the Chiquitas.

Supermarkets really get down to business at the check-out. You're right if you think they put all that candy on low shelves by the cash register so the kids can get at it, and you're wrong if you think the barcode readers are there to make things go quicker. Barcode readers are like your bank statement – you rarely look at them carefully. The next time you're at the check-out, keep your eyes firmly fixed on the digital display. That tube of Crest toothpaste probably shouldn't cost $16.95 and come up under meat/poultry. According to *Consumer Reports*, supermarkets will make between three and 11 errors in barcoding per hundred items, errors seldom in your favor. Even more insidious is the fact that barcode readers also monitor the speed of the check-out clerk – if you're not whacking that stuff through fast enough, you're toast.

Of course, you can always shop at the little place around the corner. You'll pay twice as much for everything and probably wind up getting short-changed, but at least you won't have to listen to the music.

Death Rays

(Orson Welles Dementia)

THE PARANOID CERTAINTY:
"Aliens are trying to fry my brain."

THE FACILE REASSURANCE:
"I don't have a pacemaker so what's the problem?"

THE OBJECTIVE TRUTH:

A ha! Caught you napping. It's not aliens, it's the electrical company. We are surrounded by death rays or, at the very least, an almost infinite number of man-made electromagnetic fields that are zapping us as we speak, play, watch TV, or cuddle up under the electric blanket.

I'm talking microwaves, folks, a monster that makes the drooling thing from the *Aliens* movies look like a pussycat. Before the invention of radar and the development of ultra-shortwave radio frequencies, microwave and general electromagnetic pollution didn't amount to much, unless you wound up in the hot seat at Sing Sing.

Now it's everywhere: electric razors, hair-dryers, electric blankets, boom boxes, microwave ovens, cable TV satellites, emission-control chips in your car, airport radar, fax machines, TV sets and computers. You simply can't avoid it, and it's killing you.

Since the introduction of radar during World War II, the incidence of primary brain tumors among military radio operators has risen by more than 80 percent; genetic abnormalities, sterility and Alzheimer's disease among air-traffic controllers have gone up by 300 percent.

Okay, so you don't operate a radar set, but do you live around an electrical transmission tower? They have a different name for the monster here – it's called ELF, or extremely low frequency radiation. A 65-MHz tower can cause dizziness, chronic fatigue, increased risk of cancer, miscarriage, and genetic problems – not to mention an increase in suicides directly related to proximity to these towers.

Fine, there's no transmission tower in your back-yard, so you're safe, right? Wrong. Try on a new disease and see how it fits: EHS – electromagnetic hypersensitivity syndrome. A lot of people were skeptical about this at first, but the Environmental Health Center in Dallas, Texas has confirmed that not only does EHS exist, but it is pandemic in every major

urban center, and a steadily growing problem. The symptoms of EHS are dizziness, nausea, fatigue, skin rashes, irritability, increasing anxiety close to sources of electromagnetic waves, chronic headaches, spontaneous abortion and excruciatingly painful neuralgia.

At first EHS was hard to identify because it had many of the same symptoms as asbestosis and various food allergies, but a number of tests eventually isolated it. In some people it becomes so bad that even using the telephone is painful. If you have EHS you're going to have to avoid TVs, computers, stereos, fluorescent lights, electric heaters, automatic doors and burglar alarms.

There is some evidence that an increasing level of man-made electrical fields is responsible for the upsurge of chronic fatigue syndrome (CFS), or Epstein-Barr syndrome. Silicon Valley in California has a high rate of CFS; it's also an area subjected to roughly 50 times the medically approved tolerance levels for ambient electrical fields. There is also evidence that the genetic abnormality that makes some people particularly susceptible to AIDS came about as a result of mutations caused by long-term exposure to microwaves and other forms of electromagnetic radiation.

Risk, of course, increases with exposure and proximity. Electric razors aren't really dangerous, but if you have a facial mole your risk of contracting a melanoma increases.

A new car pumps about three milligauss (MG) of juice into your system every time you drive – about three times the approved rate. A normal suburban home jolts you with a constant one-three G, but that can increase if it's close to one of those benign-looking grey boxes with the "Danger: High Voltage" stickers on it.

TV sets put out a whole menu of death rays, including microwaves, X-rays and non-ionizing electromagnetic fields, through a unique little device called a "fly-back" circuit. A 13-inch color TV puts out a level of radiation

above and beyond what's allowed at anything under a 42-inch viewing distance. A 24-inch set requires at least five feet to be safe, and one of those wall-size units should be viewed from the neighbor's yard. (As far as I know no one has studied the effect of TV radiation on the strippers in sports bars who dance nude in front of 400-inch projection screens.)

Computers put out even more radiation than TV sets. With a TV set you get fried only if you sit directly in front of it; but a computer zaps you from the left side as well, as that's where the power supply is usually located. A Macintosh, by the way, puts out a little bit more juice than an IBM, one point in favor of "Big Blue".

Fluorescent lights, while environmentally and economically correct, put out three times as much radiation as a computer, and the amount increases with every foot of tubing. As fluorescent lighting is usually located directly overhead, guess where all those nasty rays are hitting?

See that electric clock/radio, squatting evilly six inches from your pillow? Ten times the radiation of a TV set – and you're getting it for eight hours a night. For most of us, the 50 MG of radiation pumped out by a

hair-dryer isn't a big problem as we you don't use it for very long at a time, but what about the hairdresser who has one of them in hand all day every day?

Finally, of course, there is the classic emitter, the microwave oven. By and large they're safe until they start to leak, as they inevitably do. Then they can spread out a cata-strophic assortment of deadly rays: more brain tumors, increased incidence of Alzheimer's, irritability, skin problems, etc. You could always go out and buy a microwave detector, but it wouldn't do you much good as they're completely unregulated.

If you're really worried about this you can always move to a rural area in a small, undeveloped foreign country, which will give you lots of leisure time to think about the 47,378 satellites up there, pouring a steady stream of radiation in your direction.

CAFFEINE

(Juan Valdez Tic)

THE PARANOID CERTAINTY:
"Without my morning coffee I'm useless."

THE FACILE REASSURANCE:
"I'll be fine if I stick to decaf."

THE OBJECTIVE TRUTH:

E ven the most ardent tofu aficionados have tried to squirm out of this one, telling themselves that coffee is okay as long as it's been "naturally" decaffeinated, or grown on a politically correct mountainside in Colombia. Wrong.

A shabby little tree that originally came from Ethiopia, coffee has been around for a thousand years or so. It got its first boost from a Muslim sect that used it as part of a religious ritual. Eventually it found its way into Europe, and finally became the most popular addictive drug in the world.

We all know that caffeine in coffee causes nervous jitters as well as insomnia. It is also responsible for 85 percent of the chronic indigestion in the United States. It's no coincidence that the world's largest supplier of coffee also manufactures the top three antacids. Do we sense a conspiracy here? Coffee is also known to be a cause of pancreatic cancer, ulcers, and a wide variety of birth defects, including spina bifida and anancephaly (being born without a brain).

But coffee is only the tip of the iceberg. A lot of health-conscious New

> # Half an ounce of chocolate contains as much caffeine as a double espresso.

Agers have switched from coffee to oh, say, "Morning Thunder" herbal tea. Surprise, it has 50 percent more caffeine in it than your basic Folger's crystals. It also contains mate, a powerful and potentially dangerous stimulant. (The same is true of guarana powder, sold as a "brain" pill. Brain is right – it rots the brain and deep fries the old grey cells with enough caffeine to give Timothy Leary pause. Guarana, sometimes sold as "Zoom" and "Zing", is the basic ingredient for the most popular soft drink in Brazil and is now being fiercely marketed in North America and Europe as a health drink.)

Don't bother switching to regular tea, either. Your orange pekoe has as much caffeine as coffee, and great dollops of fusil oil, the wildly toxic trace element they filter out of vodka so you don't go blind. Anacin has 32 mg of caffeine per tablet, Exedrin has 64 mg and Midol has 32 mg. A 12-ounce can of Coke has a whopping 65 mg; Dr. Pepper has 61 mg; Pepsi has a mere 46 mg. The nefarious Bivarin, a headache pill you can buy over the counter, contains an astounding 200 mg per tablet. Chocolate is one of the most insidious forms of caffeine. Not only does a half-ounce square contain as much of the drug as a double espresso, it also pushes several fats and huge quantities of sugar. So beware the deadly street-corner pusher of steaming hot cocoa. Heaven knows where an addiction to Quik or Brown Cow might lead. Caffeine is a brown, steaming, and pungently aromatic slippery slope. You have been warned.

Weddings

(Bride's Enigma)

THE PARANOID CERTAINTY:
"This is all a terrible mistake."

THE FACILE REASSURANCE:
"This is the happiest day of my life."

THE OBJECTIVE TRUTH:

This most democratic of paranoias cuts across almost every social and economic stratum, choosing its victims at random. Brides, grooms, fathers, mothers, new in-laws — all have different fears relating to this happy event.

Every couple approaching their wedding day has a damn good chance of blowing the whole thing. In the United States marriages have a failure rate of one in two. In the United Kingdom it's one in three. In California, for instance, the odds against your marriage succeeding are so high that, statistically speaking, you might as well forget the tuxedo rental and cancel the reception at Howard Johnson's.

But forget the marriage for the moment and concentrate on the wedding. You're on enemy turf. Her father doesn't really like you, no matter what he says. He knows that, if you haven't already tested the nuptial waters, you're going to be doing nasty things to his daughter within hours. You'll feel his eyes boring into your back as he contemplates his daughter's fate at your calloused hands, not to mention the huge bill for feeding your relatives and ne'er-do-well friends.

Financially, of course, weddings are a disaster. The average wedding party for 100 guests costs around $15,000. Add an expensive dress, flowers from exotic locales, and a reception that serves something more than chicken-à-la-king and you're looking at $25,000–$30,000 thousand dollars. Middle-class British honeymooners go to Spain, and oddly, to Miami (40 percent). Cost: around $8,000. Preferred U.S. honeymoon destinations are Bermuda, for East Coast newlyweds, and Hawaii, from the West Coast. Both will set you back about $10M. No one really goes to Niagara Falls these days (3 percent), which may be why, for 39 bucks a night, you can get a room with a vibrating bed, mirrored ceiling, complimentary breakfast, and a pass to the Ripley's Believe It Or Not Museum, where you can contemplate your new partner and the two-headed calf fetus in the bell jar.

In the United States marriages have a failure rate of one in two, while 90 percent of elopements end in divorce.

My own casual, unscientific survey leads me to believe that no one has ever had a perfect wedding. My first wedding (admittedly an act of youthful madness) involved a blizzard, a sister-in-law-to-be attempting suicide, and a worn-out car that kept stalling on the way to the church – perhaps an omen I should have heeded. My second marriage included a heat wave, being locked out of our apartment, my new father-in-law refusing to give away his daughter, and my best man whaling the tar out of my prospective brother-in-law, who insisted that my intention was to rob his family blind and to leave my wife penniless, and the sole support of five children.

I have also heard stories of road construction accompanying the service, a Jewish wedding in which some idiot supplied a lucite tumbler for the ritual glass-breaking, any number of vomiting flower girls and ring bearers, a father dropping dead as he led his daughter up the aisle, and a groom arrested at the altar for unpaid parking tickets.

During Joan Rivers' first wedding, the rabbi's robe caught fire; Trisha Nixon's wedding cake exploded all over the guests and the band on Queen Elizabeth's tiara snapped two minutes before her wedding to Prince Philip.

Eloping isn't the answer. Ninety percent of elopements end in divorce, 45 percent in annulment. Your best chance is to be gay (85 percent success rate for a five-year relationship, 75 percent over 10 years), or inter-species.

DRUG STORES

(Paranoias Pharmacans)

THE PARANOID CERTAINTY:
"If I ask for Preparation H everyone will know."

THE FACILE REASSURANCE:
"If you can't trust your friendly neighborhood pharmacist, who can you trust?"

THE OBJECTIVE TRUTH:

It's entirely up to you, but think. Remember that scene in *It's a Wonderful Life* where the druggist accidentally gives young George Bailey the wrong prescription to deliver? In the movie George wound up with a bleeding ear and the life-long gratitude of the pharmacist. In real life it happens a lot more often than anyone dares to admit and it could cost you your life. Doctors have lousy handwriting; computers screw up (which is a whole other story); and pharmacists, after all, are only human.

Let's not even think about the disasters possible with 25,000 varieties of pills. Even non-prescription, over-the-counter goodies can get you into serious trouble.

In North America almost $4 billion a year is spent on non-prescription medications. The manufacturers spend a third again on advertising, to convince you that the stuff works. It doesn't, and some of it's downright dangerous. A full 20 percent of hospital admissions are directly related to over-the-counter drugs and, according to a U.S. National Health Institute study, 85 percent of people ignore the warnings and directions for use.

Cough syrup is 80 percent sugar, which makes it deadly for diabetics; what's left over is alcohol, making it potentially lethal for alcoholics, people on sedatives or anti-depressants, and a whole slew of allergics. Contac-C, Coricidin D and Dristan can have serious interactions with people on heart, blood pressure or asthma medication.

Antacids are another case. Flatulence and stomach aches are big business - $200 million a year, of which half is plowed back into advertising. Studies have shown that only 15 percent of antacids do what they say they do, 27 percent might have some beneficial effect and 47 percent do nothing at all.

Alka-Seltzer-type concoctions are a potpourri of things that should work, but often counteract one another. The Aspirin in the fizzy stuff will help your headache, but if you're dropping a couple of them into a glass of water to cure a hangover, look out. Aspirin aggravates the effects of alcohol on the stomach lining and can lead to intestinal bleeding. On top of that, the salt content of those two tablets is almost three times the recommended daily dose and can elevate your blood pressure. Things like Eno, Tums, and Rolaids contain calcium carbonate, an effective antacid, but one that also promotes the formation of new stomach acid, which can put some people on an endless junkie-like cycle.

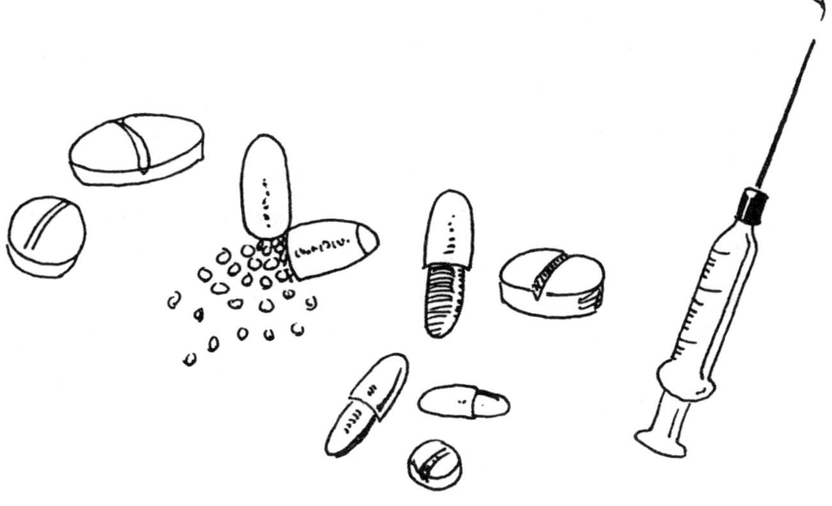

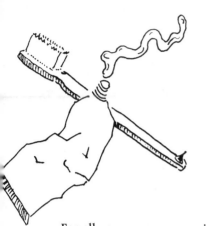

For all you younger, greasier types, watch out for anything containing that wonder-drug of the 1960s, hexaclorophine. It causes brain damage and genetic damage, and can be absorbed through the skin, causing massive infiltration into the bloodstream where it can kill off millions of beneficial bacteria. It's been pretty much banned in North America except in preparations like Physoderm – and feminine hygiene spray (use *that* stuff and you wind up with nether regions that smell like a lilac bush and a yeast infection). And, by the by, the antibacterial agent used in most deodorant soaps can cause liver damage and kidney stones, and damage the central nervous system.

Mouthwash is totally useless except to mask real illnesses, such as serious dental problems, enlarged tonsils, stomach cancer, and kidney problems. Most mouthwashes are also full of alcohol, dangerous in itself, but they also act as an astringent on your tissues – destroying beneficial bacteria and leaving you vulnerable to any number of throat ailments.

Deodorants are definitely on the no-no list as well. Some contain an antibiotic called neomycin, which can cause chronic skin irritation and rashes. Zirconium, another favorite ingredient, can cause small, usually benign growths. Inhale it (if you're still using aerosols) and you put yourself at risk for half a dozen different lung diseases. If it puts lumps on your armpits, imagine what it does to your lungs! Soap completely neutralizes most deodorants, so any soap residue will nix the roll-on. Anything containing benzylkonium oxide will rot your shirt right out from under you.

Most wart-removal compounds contain the same stuff they use to embalm corpses.

Athlete's foot? The best cure for this is fresh air. All the products available work to stop the athlete's foot, but set you up for another infection.

And just to put your mind at rest, avoid the Insomnia Trap. All of those Sleepz-It, Doz-All, and Snuz compounds you see advertised on TV don't work. Not don't work well or don't work on some people – they just plain don't work. What all these potions do well is rob you of REM, or dream sleep. The more you take, the less you dream, and the worse you sleep. Chronic lack of REM can lead to increased paranoia, psychosis, and sociopathic behavior, including murder.

A handy rule of thumb is a simple rule of advertising: the harder the pitch, the wider the curve. Except for the stuff the doctor ordered (which has problems of its own) almost everything except corn plasters and bandages are right out of an old-fashioned medicine show.

Wait. I take that back. Some bandages – the ones with no ventilating holes and some of the spray-on ones – promote infection and can cause blood poisoning.

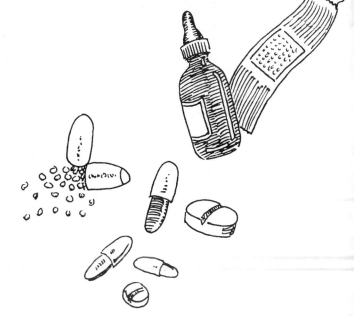

32

SSENDEDNAH-TFEL

LEFT-HANDEDNESS
(Gaucheophobia sinisterii)

THE PARANOID CERTAINTY:
"The entire world conspires against people who are left-handed."

THE FACILE REASSURANCE:
"Raise your right hand and swear to tell the truth . . ."

THE OBJECTIVE TRUTH:

The anti-left conspiracy is everywhere – telephone cords on the right that tangle up the leftie, ring binders making it impossible for the left-handed student to write, scissors that don't work, cars with controls on the right, nuts and screws that only work clockwise, and last but not least, the ubiquitous can opener that is virtually impossible for a southpaw to use.

Small potatoes you say? Think again. Seventy percent of people with insomnia are left-handed, and lefties account for more than 80 percent of migraine headache sufferers. The left-handed person is also more likely to get conjunctivitis, asthma, dermatitis, and a whole slew of other allergic problems. Forty percent of all alcoholics are left-handed, and 86 percent of left-handed alcoholics in therapy fell off the wagon within six months, against only 29 percent of right-handed alcoholics. Three times as many lefties suffer from chronic depression as do right-handed people, and four times as many commit suicide.

A recent California study also concluded that left-handed people die younger than right-handers. The average leftie lives nine years less than the average right-hander. This may well be because the vast majority of

accident victims are left-handed. A left-hander using a drill press has to bring his arm across his field of vision, a leftie using a band-saw has the safety guide on the wrong side, and a left-hander using a circular saw must rest his right hand close to the blade for support. Offices, workshops, and even cities are laid out with a clockwise bias to accommodate the right-hander. A recent study at the University of British Columbia (famous for research into handedness) showed that, in sport, work, home, tools and driving, the left-hander was 89 percent more likely than a right-hander to have an accident-related injury requiring medical attention.

Left-handers account for only 10 percent of the population and there is virtually no research and development on non-handed equipment, machinery or vehicles. In 1992 the U.S. Supreme Court ruled that an accident caused because a left-hander had to use right-handed machinery was not due to the employer's negligence, but to the employee's "deficiency". Right on!

We could go on endlessly about this, of course; every leftie can tell you about the inadequacies of fish forks, the dangers of hot water taps being on the right, and the psychological problems of being a left-handed lover with a right-handed partner. (The simple physiology of right-hand/left-hand sex is mind-boggling.)

You can try training yourself to be a rightie, but it won't work and will probably put you in therapy. Ambidextrous people are, of course, even more confused than the average southpaw. If you're into New Age Woo-Woo stuff you can also drive yourself crazy worrying about linguistic conundrums (left-handed compliments, gauche, sinister . . .) and theological (The Blessed shall sit on the Right Hand of God, Lucifer is left-handed . . .).

If I were you I'd forget the whole thing and become a writer: the only major piece of modern technology designed by a left-handed person was the typewriter.

NUCLEAR DISASTER

(Chernobylophobia)

THE PARANOID DELUSION:
"Any second now I'm going to glow in the dark."

THE ACCEPTED REALITY:
*"The Environmental Protection Agency is on our side.
We have nothing to worry about."*

THE OBJECTIVE TRUTH:

The Cold War is over. Now we can all stop worrying about Nuclear War, a sooty, century-long winter, and nasty isotopes in breast milk. Hardly. The first weapons-grade uranium and plutonium were manufactured in the Pacific northwestern U.S. about half a century ago. The waste from those first bombs is still there, buried under a few tons of sand on the floodplain of the Columbia River. Since then the United States, the United Kingdom, the Soviet Union, France, and a few other places have manufactured around 165,000 nuclear warheads. As well, the world's 765 nuclear reactors pump 550,000 tons of high-grade waste a year. Then there are the 90,000 tons of radioactive isotopes manufactured annually for medical use. You can also factor in the 220,000 tons of high-grade fissionable products that get shipped around the world each year.

There must be rules for all that waste, you say? No. Only a protocol for who's going to lie to whom. The Hanford Nuclear Reservation in Washington State stores nuclear waste from around the world; half their storage tanks are leaking into the Columbia, killing off the downstream salmon fishery. They refer to accidents at the facility as "incidents", and measure radioactive contamination in "sunshine units". Therefore, it's "sunshine units" causing all those cancers, not radiation sickness.

Were "incidents" like Three Mile Island and Chernobyl exceptions? No, they weren't. At Hanford there have been more than 1,600 incidents during the past 10 years, 400 at the Windscale complex in the United Kingdom, and who knows how many in what was the Soviet Union. There are three nuclear waste dumps within 100 miles of London, England, and a total of 412 waste depositories in the United States storing nuclear garbage. The stuff is regularly shipped around the country in trucks, airplanes, and freight cars that rarely have radiation warning stickers on them. One freight car full of nasty material from Three Mile Island was lost on a siding in Wisconsin for three and a half months. Every year 1,200 people die as a direct result of nuclear "incidents", and tens of thousands of cancers are waste-related.

And it's going to get worse. All those war-heads the Russians and Americans are dismantling have to wind up somewhere, and the most likely spot is your back-yard. Buy a Geiger counter and invest in lead futures.

At the Hanford Nuclear Reservation in Washington State, radioactive contamination is measured in "sunshine units."

ADVER

THE PARANOID CERTAINTY!
"Maybe it's my breath."

THE FACILE REASSURANCE!
"They have laws about that . . . don't they?"

THE OBJECTIVE TRUTH!

Well, yes and no. There are rules about what you can and cannot say in advertisements. There are even rules about truth in advertising, but by and large advertising agencies are self-policed. This is like allowing the Pentagon to approve its own budgets.

Since the first bootmaker hung out his shingle there have been two basic elements in advertising – sex and fear. Fear advertising works best during periods of sustained crisis, preferably war. People being killed on distant shores have always been good for business. Take an issue of *The London Illustrated News* from September 1940. **"IT MAY BE YOU!"** trumpets an ad on the back page. The photograph shows a man looking as if he's just been released from Gestapo interrogation. The cause of his pain? PYORRHEA! Just like four out of five readers of the magazine.

It's almost a sure bet that all your teeth are going to fall out unless you use Forhan's toothpaste. But wait! Here's Phillips Dental Magnesia (the same stuff you take for a stomach ache, except you're supposed to brush your teeth with this version) announcing that they are waging **WAR ON DINGY TEETH.**

SPECTACLE WEARERS! – Your eyes need extra care, especially in war time. The advertisement for an eyedrop solution never explains why people who wear glasses suffer more during the blitz.

Or, **WHICH IS IT TO BE?! ROTTING WOOD OR GOOD SOUND TIMBER?! THE ANSWER LIES IN YOUR HANDS!** – and a drop of Solignum Wood Preservative. Beside that little warning is an advisory from the Rednutt Sherry

TISING!

folks: as transport can be a little erratic these days why not buy two bottles the next time – just in case a U-boat sinks the next shipment.

How about, **MEET DANGER WITH LIPS THAT ARE GLAMOROUS!** Flogging lipstick to the Resistance, perhaps? Some advertisers went a bit too far: **WHAT ABOUT GASES THAT BURN THE FLESH?!** was accompanied by a picture of a petrified teenager in a gas mask in an attempt to sell a face cream called Benutrum. One of the more sinister ads was for Fortiphone Hearing Aids: **WITHOUT FORTIPHONE YOU MAY NOT HEAR THE ALERT!** Evidently you wouldn't see hundreds of people rushing to shelters or feel bombs exploding all around you.

After the war, sex became the prime mover in advertising, but fear didn't vanish altogether. There was the Eveready ad showing someone bleeding at the foot of the basement stairs with a dead flashlight just out of reach: "He didn't buy Eveready." Thousands of women were severely traumatized because they weren't using Kotex belts and therefore bulged in places they shouldn't. Wincing men in boxer shorts apparently had the opposite problem – and stared enviously at the changing-room studs in Jockeys.

The Vietnam War didn't do much for retail sales, but ads in the big military hardware magazines were way up: **"Rank Passive Night Sights – Better by far than a shot in the dark."** But the gold star goes to General Dynamics for their classic: **"Killability! The true test of Target Acquisition Systems!"**

By the late 1960s life was becoming more complex with thought control and subliminal advertising – so much so that it was rumored that laws controlling subversive advertising methods were in the works. Maybe, but they were never enacted. To this day dozens of large corporations use the technique regularly. There are also a number of companies using "mood" music to make people buy more, and the lighting and furniture design of most fast-food outlets are specifically geared to making sure that you buy more and eat faster. The newest form of this type of thing is an odor system geared to human pheromones, which sets you up for euphoric shopping.

You can bet your designer boots that this is only the tip of the iceberg. Commercials already cost far more than TV shows. Rumor has it that Ted Turner has spent millions planning a cable channel that is nothing but commercials.

VIOLENT CRIME

(Thugee's Twitch)

THE PARANOID CERTAINTY:
"The streets just aren't safe anymore, they just said so on CNN."

THE FACILE REASSURANCE:
"You'll be fine as long as you don't look like a victim."

THE OBJECTIVE TRUTH:

The FBI Uniform Crime Reports for 1992 log 4.1 violent crimes in the United States every minute. By violent crime they mean aggravated assault, rape, murder, larceny, theft and burglary. They do not include non-sexual "body crimes" such as mugging. In New York 4,000 muggings are reported every 12 hours.

Ah, but England doesn't have a violent-crime problem, because handguns aren't a problem. Think again. The violent-crime rate in London is equal to that of Los Angeles, the only difference being that violent crime in London is strongly associated with domestic disputes. Apparently they've turned wife-beating and child abuse into a fine art.

In Germany the per-capita violent-crime rate is twice that of New York; Moscow's violent-crime rate is higher than that of the rest of Europe combined.

Don't pat yourself on the back if you've moved out into the peaceful countryside. The rate of property crime, assault and rape in rural areas in general with populations under 5,000 people per square mile is almost exactly that of larger cities; the use of handguns and rifles is triple that in urban areas.

The best way to protect yourself is to install a top-flight burglar alarm and hide under the bed. Barring that you can utilize the fire-with-fire technique. A film editor in New York devised a terrific way of getting home through Central Park late at night. He sticky-taped his entire body with strips of torn newspaper and ran through the park clucking like a demented chicken. No one came near him. Mace is good as long as you don't spritz a plainclothes cop on a stake-out. Handguns are a serious mistake; in Los Angeles there are as many accidental shooting fatalities as there are murders.

> The violent crime rate in London is equal to that of Los Angeles; in Germany the per-capita rate is twice that of New York; and if you've moved to the peaceful countryside, the use of handguns and rifles is triple that in urban areas.

The lowest crime rate in the United States is in an obscure place called Beaver, Pennsylvania; the worst per-capita violent-crime rate is in, not surprisingly, Miami, Florida. According to recent studies the worst up-and-coming crime spots are Vallejo, California, in the Napa Valley, and Kankakee, Illinois. I wouldn't move to Pine Bluff, Arizona, either; not only has it shown a steady 27 percent rise in violent crime over the past five years, it was also rated as the overall worst place to live in the United States from every possible statistical standpoint with the exception of sunshine days. Move to Pine Bluff and you'll be raped, mugged and assaulted under a cloudless sky.

TOXIC SHOCK SYNDROME

THE PARANOID CERTAINTY:
"If men got it they would have cured it years ago."

THE FACILE REASSURANCE:
"They cured it years ago."

THE OBJECTIVE TRUTH:

This one isn't funny at all.

No, they didn't. It just stopped being front-page news. Toxic shock syndrome (TSS) is caused by a normally benign little bug called *Staphylococcus aureus*, which most men and women carry around in large quantities. It usually lives in the nasal passages, on the skin and in the vagina. Every once in a while, for no apparent reason, *Staph A*, as it's known to its friends, turns mean, multiplies like crazy and secretes a life-threatening toxin. Before 1980 the result, toxic shock syndrome, was virtually unknown; then researchers noticed that people, mostly young, menstruating women, were dying . . . of something.

It took a long time for researchers to track down that something, but they did: the women were being killed by tampons.

Then came the big surprise: they suddenly found themselves taking on the incredibly remunerative feminine-napkin industry. Like death and dying, menstruation doesn't fluctuate with general economics. Every month, even during a recession, 85 million North American women buy 941 million tampons and sanitary pads. Big, big business, but never enough for the Big Three of tampons – Kimberley-Clark, Procter and Gamble, and Johnson and Johnson.

Which brings us back to TSS. In 1980 all three companies decided that all those women needed the added aggravation of even more choice in tampons and napkins and introduced "Super-Absorbent" products – all at the same time. They even put the same chemicals in them, chemicals that provided a perfect breeding ground for *Staph A*. Some women died; a lot more got sick. After a few multi-million-dollar lawsuits were quietly settled out of court, all three companies cut back on the chemicals.

Did this make TSS go away? No, but it forced the companies to put tiny information notices on the already small-print instruction sheets in each box. The notices advise that use of super-absorbent tampons and napkins has been shown to "contribute" to toxic shock – like a charity donation.

> It took a long time to discover that women were being killed by tampons.

Beaten but not defeated they took all those chemicals and developed another product to give women more choice, of course. Lo and behold, the panty-liner was born and women all over the Western world were inundated with advertising that gently insisted they worry about "tell-tale" odor. (That gave the companies yet another idea – the deodorant tampon – which adds a few more medical problems.)

As any good doctor will tell you, genuine odor during menstruation is probably a signal that there is something seriously wrong; the deodorant simply keeps you from finding that out. There is no such thing as "tell-tale" odor. So, panty-liners have no positive function and they're downright dangerous. Because they are made of cellulose, like tampons, they introduce oxygen into the vagina, which can cause chronic yeast infections. Now, boys and girls, which companies own the largest manufacturers of yeast-infection topical medicines? Very good.

Since the Big Three are also the major suppliers of disposable diapers, it stood to reason that super-absorbent chemicals might be useful here, too. Did they stop to consider that a little girl in a super-absorbent diaper is just as vulnerable to TSS as her mom? In fact, more so, as TSS occurs primarily among young people who haven't developed a tolerance for *Staph A*.

You think you've beaten the system, right? Wrong. Those potentially fatal chemicals will soon be showing up in incontinence products for the elderly. You can bet your life on it.

P E T S

(Gravy Train Dementia)

THE PARANOID CERTAINTY:
"I'm starting to look exactly like my dachshund."

THE FACILE REASSURANCE:
"Pets are a wonderful way for children to learn about nurturing and responsibility."

THE OBJECTIVE TRUTH:

Better to spend a fortune on a stuffed giraffe from F.A.O. Schwartz than spend five minutes at the pound. Your children will tug desperately on your pant leg and look up at you with that mournful stare. You'll give in. An hour later some wretched creature will be testing out the Scotchguard and throwing up on the duvet, and your children will have vanished. Nor will they be around to take Fido for his twice-daily walk, or change Fluffy's litter. They certainly won't be around when the vet bill comes sliding through the mail slot, insisting that you cough up for the claw clipping, flea bath, deworming and ear drops.

My FAMILY plays host to two birds of indeterminate sex, a large and extremely neurotic cat who regularly mistakes the bathmat for his litter box, and an eighteen-hundred-pound arab/quarter horse cross with shoes more expensive than my son's Nike Airs and a dentist's bill to match. The birds doo-doo in the bedroom, screech, and fling cracked seed remnants all over the kitchen. The cat refuses to get out of my chair, sharpens his claws on any vertical surface, and makes macabre moaning sounds in the middle of the night. The nag's carrot habit has nearly bankrupted me, and the horse accoutrements that get ferried around in the car leave everything, my daughter included, smelling like a barn.

Pets aren't just expensive and time-consuming, they are a massive social disaster. Each and every day, in North America, dogs and cats deposit 10,000 tons of feces and 500,000 gallons of urine. Think about that for a minute. In the U.K. the daily average is about 492 tons of doggie-doo and 118,878 gallons of urine.

The cost of keeping pets? Astronomical. In 1992 $4.6 billion was spent on pets in the United States. The average cat costs $550 a year, the average dog almost $700. On top of that you can add $750 million for public animal control and $200 million for disposal of pet remains. Dog bites are second only to gonorrhea as a health problem, with three million bites reported at a cost of $100 million per year to treat.

Somewhere out there, 85 billion fleas lurk, waiting to dig into our ankles. Then there's toxoplasmosis, which favors the human spinal cord, brain and eyes. Half a billion people have got it – and almost all of them caught it from dogs and cats. *Toxocara canis*, or roundworm, can cause blindness in humans. It is often misdiagnosed as cancer. Ninety-three percent of newborn puppies have the disease, which is rampantly infectious. It changes into something even more lethal in humans – visceral larval migrans. Let us not forget creeping eruption, hookworm, tapeworm and *Diplopylidium caninum*.

We also have to deal with the fact that dogs – all 27 million of them in the U.S. – can also carry leptospirosis, which permanently damages liver and kidneys; rabies, which can kill you; ringworm; the aforementioned fleas; rocky mountain spotted fever, a variant of typhoid; and scabies. In case you think that I've got it in for the pooch population, add cat scratch fever, a form of encephalitis; cryptococcosis, a fungus infection incredibly difficult to get rid of in people; *Giardia lamblia*, a cat-spread form of dysentery; and, according to one British study, multiple sclerosis. Birds, bless their feathery little breasts, can give us all psittacosis, or Parrot Fever.

There is only one way: stop this before it starts. Take your children to the video store, rent *Old Yeller*, and force them to watch it over and over, especially the scene in which Yeller has to be put down. As an alternative, rent *The Godfather* and put the horse-in-the-bed sequence on an endless video loop. Your children will hate you, but you'll all be richer for the experience.

AGIN

(Dorian Gray Dementia)

THE PARANOID CERTAINTY:
"I'm turning into my mother."

THE FACILE REASSURANCE:
"Now I can relax and enjoy my Golden Years."

THE OBJECTIVE TRUTH:

D eep in your secret self you know, without a shadow of doubt, that you are going to be the first person who lives forever. There's no need to be embarrassed. All of us think the same thing.

At some point, usually in our late teens or early twenties, we declare a chronological full stop. Sadly, our bodies and pension funds don't notice.

Once upon a time the guys over at Kimberley-Clark spent all their time coming up with new "feminine hygiene" products for a seemingly ever-expanding market of menstruating women, and an equally inventive line of diapers. Now those researchers are designing incontinence pants. This is no joke; the tampon/sanitary napkin industry in the United States employs almost 100,000 people and generates more than $7 billion a year. By 2010, 75 percent of that market will have disappeared in a puff of estrogen. We'll save a few trees, but lose a lot of jobs.

True, life expectancy has risen dramatically since 1900, but quality of life after the age of 65 has declined. The hundred-thousand-dollar life insurance policy you paid for years ago won't buy one of your kids a year of university education these days; the interest income won't put new tires on the RV. That house you scrimped for is steadily losing its value, no matter what the real estate people tell you. During the next 20 years your single-family suburban house with four bedrooms and a den will turn into a white elephant. By the year 2000 the median age of the Western world's population is going to be over 50. We'll all be downsizing into easy-maintenance apartments with elevators, ramps, and on-call nursing.

If you're a true Baby Boomer, born between 1946 and 1960, you've already got early symptoms. Hair is thinning or gone, stomach muscles are sagging and you've stopped making jokes about Oil of Olay. The only people getting rich are the plastic surgeons doing tummy tucks, ear pulls and collagen injections, none of which have real long-term benefits.

Forget Iron John. The male Boomer's sex drive is declining. So is his stamina, angle and firmness. Boomer women are beginning to produce too little estrogen and too much testosterone: things are either drying up or growing a mustache.

Adding insult to injury are the inescapable demographics. In the year 2010, when the first Boomer wave hits 65, Social Security in the United States is going to pay out $37 billion. Within five years the bill will climb to $1.1 trillion, more than the present annual deficit of the United States. And it's no better elsewhere. The only way to keep all of us out of the poor-house is to make sure some of us die faster. Avoiding recession and resisting the temptation to deficit-finance with the pension pot would help, too.

Demographers conclude that what we really need is a really big war, or an updated Black Death. The problem is there aren't enough up-and-coming workers to service all of us OFWAFs – Old Fogeys Without A Future. The big war would cut into the already dwindling labor supply.

The only bright light on the horizon is another inescapable statistic: by the year 2050 most of the Boomers will be dead.

It's a start.

JUNK FOOD
(Ingredientsis nauseam)

THE PARANOID CERTAINTY:
"I have this secret addiction to Oreos."

THE FACILE REASSURANCE:
"Well, at least they can't do anything to freshly ground pepper."

THE OBJECTIVE TRUTH:

Most people know that junk food is bad, but they eat it anyway. I mean, do you really care about hydrogenated versus non-hydrogenated fats? Do you really check the and/or listings and wonder what the "or" might be?

The "or" you're likely to find in Oreos is probably beef fat, which is made by boiling down the carcasses of dead cows until they look like something from a Dresden bomb shelter. That creamy filling has nothing, repeat nothing, in common with dairy products. It's half beef fat and half sugar, with a bit of air whipped in for good measure. By the way, most of the cookies you buy in the local 7/Eleven have a shelf life of up to 10 years. Imagine that, biting into a Fig Newton manufactured back in the disco era; history lives at the supermarket.

Ah, maraschino cherries – the little red and green flecks you find in Christmas cakes, the red nubbins floating in the can of fruit cocktail, the blob on top of your ice cream sundae.

A pox on Mr. Maraschino, whoever he was. The cherries are chosen entirely on the basis of their stems' ability to stay stuck in the fruit under conditions that would defeat a platoon of Marines. First, they are put into a bath of bleach for three to six weeks until all color has been drained out of them and they look like eyeballs with stems. They are then rinsed in a

solution of alum and more bleach just to make
sure anything even vaguely natural has been
destroyed. Then they're dropped into a tank of red
dye and left to sit for a month or more. When the
cherries have achieved the color of a traffic light
they're passed along to another tank, filled with
glucose syrup heated to boiling. They boil in the syrup
for 20 to 30 hours and then go back into the dying tank
for another two-week run. Then you eat them.

The pimentos you find in most olives aren't pimento at all, but so far
research has failed to pin down exactly what those little red blobs are. The
best guess is some sort of cellulose compound, but I'm betting that they're
cast-offs from the maraschino cherry people.

The worst offenders are the seasonings. That's right, the innocuous
little bottles in the spice department that couldn't hurt a fly. Well, they
have hurt the odd fly because that's what you often find in them. The Food
and Drug people even have permissible numbers of insect parts that are
allowed in various spices. Curry powder is allowed 100 insect fragments
per 25 grams and pepper 50 fragments per 100 grams. Salt is allowed
three maggot eggs per pound.

Coffee? ten percent of all coffee may contain as many as 500 insect
fragments per pound. Apple butter is allowed 25 full insects (ground up,
mind you) in each 16-ounce jar; peanut butter is allowed up to 650 insect
fragments per 12-ounce jar, and the people who make Skippy's Extra
Chunky are even allowed one rodent hair per 100 grams. Orange juice will
contain at least 10 fruit fly eggs or two fly maggots per can, and tomato
juice is crawling with all sorts of things, from drosophila maggots to thrips.

The creamy stuff in Twinkies and other "cakes" wrapped in cellophane
is actually rendered lard. Hot dogs have occasionally been found to contain
bits and pieces of Rover and Fido. Chocolate milk (usually called chocolate
"Drink") is actually a cleaning process used to scour the dairy pipes at the
end of the shift. They use cocoa powder as the abrasive and whoosh it
through the plumbing, then collect the sludgy result at the other end.

I could go on, but I've lost my appetite.

48

Your Car

(Angstis automobilia)

THE PARANOID CERTAINTY:
"Driving these days is like jogging blindfolded through a minefield."

THE FACILE REASSURANCE:
"The airbag and the anti-lock brakes will save me."

THE OBJECTIVE TRUTH:

Slightly more than 49 million automobiles were sold world-wide in 1992. Add these to the 245 million cars already on the road and you get 294 million large, dangerous, metal objects – one for every 20 people on the planet.

Or consider this: in the United States alone there are 14 million drivers over the age of 75, 10 million drivers under the age of 19, and 17 million drivers between 19 and 24. That's 41 million drivers who have the reaction time of a three-toed sloth or delusions of immortality that would give Saddam Hussein a run for his money. This does not bode well for careful, thoughtful and experienced drivers like you and me.

Of the 43,500 automobile fatalities in the United States in 1992, slightly more than half were alcohol-related. Two out of three occurred on the highway, and 53 percent took place at night. (Avoid late-night visits to Aunt Mabel's farm.) Twelve thousand of these deaths resulted from impacting with a fixed object, five out of six of them in rural areas, mostly at night. What are these late-night lunatics running into? Unfortunately, there are no equivalent statistics on cow and moose fatalities.

If you're relying on seat belts or airbags to save you, think again. Not one major Western country has a national seat-belt law. Of the 1.5 million automobile accidents in the United States causing permanent disabling injury, 940,000 were rear-end collisions in which airbags wouldn't have helped. Airbags work at less than 60 percent efficiency. Unless you're a crash-test dummy you stand a pretty good chance of getting a face full of corn-starch airbag lubricant just before the other guy's hood ornament comes through the windshield.

(Rinky's Dink Dementia)

THE PARANOID CERTAINTY:
"It's too small/can't satisfy her/her other lovers were all hung like moose/she has fantasies about Long Dong Silver."

THE FACILE REASSURANCE:
"It's not size, it's skill."

THE OBJECTIVE TRUTH:
Of 132 sex manuals consulted, all list penis size in the index, and all tell you that size doesn't matter. Almost all were written by men.

Don't be a fool. Of course size matters. Anyone with any experience at all knows that sex and friction swell hand in hand (so to speak). Sure, sure, a woman's vagina has major nerve bundles for only the first two and a half inches of its length, and maximum clitoral pressure can be achieved through inventive positioning. Pay no attention. Women can tell the difference. While thickness is probably more important than length, the former is usually a function of the latter. The longer the thicker, the thicker the better.

Most sex manuals measure the average dong at 5 1/2 to 6 1/2 inches in length and 2 1/2 to 3 1/2 inches in circumference. What they don't tell you is that the average woman's vagina can stretch to 11 1/2 inches in length and 18-1/2 inches in circumference – think of a two-quart keg of German beer and you'll be in the ball park.

For the most part women tend to be diplomatic about penis size, but they're just being kind. According to a recent survey most women over 30 have had between 15 and 25 sexual partners, so she'll probably have met one smaller than yours. She'll probably also have had one in the giant zucchini range.

*The Atlas of Human Sexual Anatomy (*2nd Edition*)* describes (and illustrates) the wiener of one John D., which measures a whopping 16 2/3 inches erect, with a circumference of 9 3/4 inches. The semi-anonymous John is probably one of the few men in the world not paranoid about the size of his penis. He may know some of the women you do. Try not to think about it.

NUCLEAR WAR

(Strangelove's Gavotte)

THE PARANOID CERTAINTY:
"Armageddon is only 15 minutes away."

THE FACILE REASSURANCE:
"Nuclear war is a thing of the past."

THE OBJECTIVE TRUTH:

Depending on where you live, nuclear barbecuing may be just six minutes away. If you live in the U.K., it's four minutes; anywhere in Europe, it's two sneezes and a walk to the bathroom.

The chances of nuclear war have actually increased since peace broke out. Most of us thought about nuclear war in terms of the United States and the Soviet Union. Most of us think the threat ended with the cold war. Most of us are crazy.

There are 426 facilities in the United States containing nuclear bombs, another 96 in foreign countries, and several fleets of nuclear submarines skulking the seven seas. Only four of the United States' do not host nuclear missiles. In the former Soviet Union there are three times that many missile facilities and almost twice as many individual warheads, although the total kilotonnage is about the same.

In the United States and the U.K., the command and control for these missiles is run through the local telephone lines. In whatever the Soviet Union is called now, command and control are done by telex. The potential for disaster is enormous. Flocks of geese have activated these systems, and now, with all the missiles threading through computers, we may be at the mercy of an errant chip manufactured in the suburbs of Osaka. And these are the countries we can officially monitor. Then there're the other guys. Don't kid yourself, somewhere in the desert old Saddam Hussein is putting together his own version of the Doomsday Bomb, and so are the folks in 54 other countries. Brazil has nuclear capability, so does Mexico, and Costa Rica. So do really loose cannons like South Africa and Libya.

Even scarier are the free-lance A-bombs. Consider this: you're running Ukraine; you have a huge inventory of nuclear missiles and nothing much to do with them. Some guy in a funny hat from Bosnia approaches you on a street-corner with a wad of cash. Three weeks later people are firing Scuds and Sidewinders in Montenegro. A little later, Zaire decides that it wants to take on Kenya. Gaddafi decides to go for broke and puts half a dozen hydrogen bombs on a jumbo aimed at Heathrow. Canadian natives pick up a few bombs second-hand from Estonia and do a Little Big Horn in downtown Ottawa. Washington, D.C., gets wiped out by a fringe group of nuclear-armed, born-again fundamentalists who want to make Mississippi into a Christian Theme Park.

In the last few years the world has turned into a bizarre collection of banana republics. Half of them have nuclear capability. The only way to stop the threat of nuclear war is to destroy all existing weapons (300,000 odd, at last count), destroy all documentation relating to their construction (available at your local library for six bucks' worth of photocopying) and ban all uranium and other fissionable material. Then you'll have time to look for the 6–10 kg of plutonium that go missing each year.

The best we can hope for is a giant meteor heading for Earth to use all the weapons on. One way or another they're going to be used if history is anything to go on. The Catholic Church banned the cross-bow except against infidels. Richard Nixon banned production of chemical and biological weapons – while funding their development to the tune of $55 billion a year.

Now, if we could only find a small, useless country that everyone didn't like. . . .

IMPOTENCE

(Casanova's Droop or Guilty-Wilty Disease)

THE PARANOID CERTAINTY:
"Oh, God! Maybe this means I'm gay!"

THE FACILE REASSURANCE:
"Never happens. No, really."

THE OBJECTIVE TRUTH:

If it hasn't happened yet, it will. By age 35, 90 percent of men have experienced at least one episode of impotence. Most of the time it means you've had too much to drink or you feel guilty about something. However, by age 35, 10 percent of men have primary impotence, defined as an inability to achieve an erection on four separate occasions. In these cases, the worse it gets, the worse it gets – the more you try, the less the effect.

Medical textbooks list several reasons for primary impotence among heterosexual men, including a traumatic first sexual experience, a homosexual relationship lasting more than one year, a domineering mother or father, hormonal diseases, post-surgical complications, high-blood-pressure medication, overdependence on alcohol, anti-depressants, fatigue, anxiety about finances, and poor nutrition.

Therapy at a Masters and Johnson–style clinic, which has about a 60 percent success rating, will set you back $10,000 on average. Enough to increase your anxiety – and impotence. The best cure, supposedly, is to stop worrying – just forget about it. Right. Sure. Several studies indicate that hormones used to promote growth in chickens destroy human testosterone production. This can lead to primary impotence and breast enlargement, among other scary conditions. Anabolic steroids and half a dozen other goodies you can get under the counter at the gym will do the same thing.

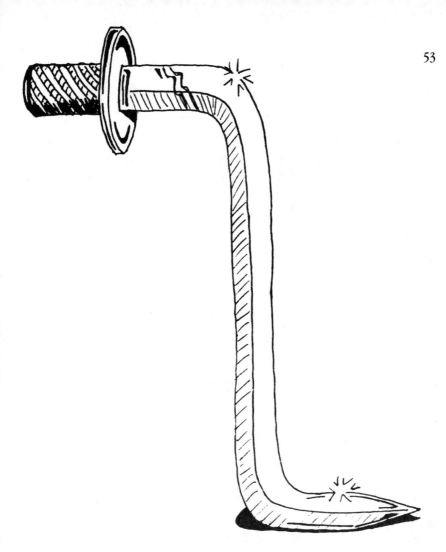

So it all comes down to this:
you become impotent because you worry.
You worry because you're impotent,
which keeps you impotent,
which causes you to worry. . . .
Now, if reading this causes you to worry, relax.
If you worry, sometime in the near future
you just might become impotent,
but it may be just a fluke,
so don't worry,
because if you worry . . .

RESTAURANT EMBARRASSMENT

(Wine Steward's Sneer)

THE PARANOID CERTAINTY:
"The maître d' is actually a Russian Prince. That's why he's looking down his nose at me."

THE FACILE REASSURANCE:
"I'm a regular here."

THE OBJECTIVE TRUTH:

Restaurosis has an almost infinite number of variations, none of them pleasant. Latent Restaurosis (LR) generally strikes while eating alone and begins with the menu. If they spell "coleslaw" "cold slaw", is the cook literate enough to read the public health notice over the grill? All those old worries about cats and egg rolls return as we visualize the slop pail. How long has the bowl of egg salad been sitting on the counter and why was there a pest-control car discreetly parked in the alley?

A variant of LR syndrome is WPR, or Weird Patron Restaurosis. With whom is the person in the booth behind you having a conversation about his ex-wife? – there's no one else eating with him. And why is he pouring a bowl of Ketchup into his saucer? Will he turn his attention to you? WPR can be compounded when everyone else in the place, the owner included, is snickering. A third variation is Newspaper Restaurosis (NR). While reading a newspaper left behind by a previous patron, you realize that all the notices in the personals advertising golden showers and rubber discipline have been circled. Oh, look, the smiling patron has come back for the forgotten tabloid.

More sophisticated Restaurosis comes with haute cuisine. Acute Restaurant Embarrassment (ARE) can come about when, after insisting on picking up the check for dinner for eight, you discover that (a) you don't have enough cash, (b) the credit card you put down comes back to you neatly sliced in half, and (c) you're going to be violently ill from the Oysters Rockefeller.

> ## The Boeuf Hâchée avec touts les condiments may be $24.95, but it's still hamburger with the works.

The first thing to remember when eating in a high-end restaurant is that these places are designed with the paranoid in mind. The entire process – being seated, ordering, eating and paying for the meal – has been programmed for anxiety. The maître d' is wearing a better suit than you are; the server is more attractive than you are, and always younger. The menu is written in an obscure foreign language, printed without prices, and often refers to people and places you've never heard of: Eggs au Buerre de Montelone d'Amafillio, or Beef Count Ravellski.

Ah, the wine list. Is it more sophisticated to order the one California wine that won't be laughed at, or the one with the French name that actually comes from a small island off Newfoundland. Going by price doesn't work: that $80 bottle of 1972 Château Chemin de Fer d'Alban is really Old Niagara jug wine from upstate New York re-labelled for Amtrak.

The same is true for the food. The Boeuf Hâchée avec touts les condiments may be $24.95, but it's still hamburger with the works.

While you're eating your overpriced meal in a dark room, served by a beautiful young man with an enormous pepper shaker, and an attitude, you may also find yourself suffering from a classic Restaurosis side effect. Is the valet parking attendant making copies of all your keys for future use? And why doesn't the baby-sitter answer the phone?

BIRTH CONTROL
(Latex Breakus Syndrome)

THE PARANOID CERTAINTY:
*"My period is an hour late. . . . I must be pregnant.
A million little spermatozoa can't be wrong."*

THE FACILE REASSURANCE:
"Don't worry, I had a vasectomy."

THE OBJECTIVE TRUTH:

He's probably fibbing. Besides, having a vasectomy is no guarantee that you won't find yourself loitering around the Pampers aisle. Vasectomies have a "leakage" rate of about 4 percent.

Oral contraceptives are safest, but you have to put up with sore breasts, mood swings, weight gain, and the possibility of uterine cancer and/or blindness, not to mention the knowledge that the pills are made from the urine of pregnant mares. The horses are kept continually pregnant, intubated, bloated with fluids and diuretics, and rarely exercised. They become prone to diabetes and blindness. If the foal is male it is generally clubbed to death on the spot.

Now that you're feeling guilty we can move on to less-effective birth control choices.

IUDs for instance. If you're using one you stand a 3-7 percent chance of getting pregnant, as well as risking both uterine punctures and tubal pregnancy. The makers of the Dalkon Shield, which looks remarkably like the villain in the 1957 horror film called *The Tingler*, are still being sued by hundreds of women even though they've declared bankruptcy. Then there're rope burns, but you'll have to ask your partner about them.

Diaphragms? A 12 percent chance of pregnancy here, mostly from taking them out too soon or putting them in too late. Condoms aren't nearly as effective as Mr. Schmidt would have you believe: 15 percent fail, even if you use them religiously (so to speak), defeated by human error, fluid hydraulics, the tensile strength of latex, and the physics of the male organ.

Coitus Interruptus (commonly known as "What are you doing to Mommy?") has a pregnancy rating of 16 percent, mostly because of his inability to interruptus before it's too late. This puts it in a dead heat with the Papal Polka.

All those foams, jellies and suppositories you see on the shelf with the surgical jelly are next to useless, leaving you with a 50-50 chance of getting pregnant. Doing nothing at all is as close as you can get – 80 percent – to preplanning a baby shower.

There are a few new options looming. The Morning After pill is effective, but so far there haven't been any long-range studies on side effects, and the Woman's Condom, inevitably referred to as French Federal Express, is so laughable that it's probably just about 100 percent effective – no one trying to put one of them on could stop herself from gales of hysterical laughter.

As well, some old wives' tales are still making the rounds:

Yes, you can get pregnant while having your menstrual period.

No, the fact that he had measles when he was 12 is no guarantee.

Vinegar doesn't work.

Look on the bright side: yes, it is possible to become pregnant without ever having done "it". Difficult, unlikely, and very bad luck, but possible nevertheless.

Jogging.

(Fixxophobia)

THE PARANOID CERTAINTY:
"I'm in such bad shape, starting to jog would probably kill me."

THE FACILE REASSURANCE:
"I'm doing my best to interface with the planet on a cardiovascular/ aerobic/ozone-friendly level. I mean, it's the least I can do."

THE OBJECTIVE TRUTH:

Fixxophobia generally affects slightly overweight men in their early 40s who pay serious attention to cereal ads selling high-fiber content. Jim Fixx, you will recall, was the happy-go-lucky doctor who popularized jogging in the early 1970s and then dropped dead in his Reeboks at the end of a workout. Fitness junkies wore black sweatbands for weeks, and Converse starting courting basketball players instead of runners.

Jogging is bad for you – did George Bush look happy as he True Gritted his way around the White House track? No. Jogging is hard on your ankles, screws up your knees, and puts smiles on chiropractors' faces as they snap your impacted vertebra back into place. It's a terrible way to get from one place to another, and you arrive all sweaty and out of breath.

Early-morning and late-night jogging get women raped and men mugged, and in Central Park men and women alike get raped. And mugged. The footwear is hideously expensive, you have to wear an idiotic fanny pack to hold your worldly wealth, and most humans look ludicrous in sweatpants. In a word, as alternative transportation or health aid, jogging sucks.

What about bicycles? In New York City there are 900 bicycle deaths a year. A "serious" bicycle can cost upwards of a thousand dollars. You have to disassemble it before parking, carrying the front wheel around with you like a Greek philosopher in search of an honest man, or someone who can put the damn thing back on.

Every man knows the incredible pain resulting from a slipped sprocket and women have known true fear as their skirts are chewed up by a gnashing chain. Fewer humans look good stuffed like sausages into bicycle pants than in sweatpants.

> It's a terrible way to get from one place to another, and you arrive all sweaty and out of breath.

Rollerblades? Just ask any good orthopedic surgeon how he paid for his new Jag. Real roller skates have four wheels on each foot (a total of eight) with a broader wheelbase than your foot. Rollerblades combine the worst elements of ice skates and concrete, and cause pedestrians and motorists to encourage you to take a header into a plate-glass window or the side of a bus.

Skateboarding, an earlier variation of rollerblading, is usually practised by hell-bent teenagers with strange haircuts and even stranger clothes. Skateboarders spend much of their time searching for empty swimming pools and parking garage ramps. "Bunking", another favorite, involves squatting to hang onto the rear bumper of your car, then looming up as you hit a red light and cutting in front of you. For anyone over the age of 16 skateboarding is probably physically impossible as it involves muscles, tendons and reaction times long gone for most of us. The worst case scenario, of course, is you hitting the kid and getting sued for everything you own.

In the end, the only real alternative form of transportation open to the average person is walking, and even that can get you into serious trouble. In the United States 7,000 pedestrians are killed each year while in basic walk mode; another 2,200 die of exposure. So until someone perfects the Star Trek Transporter you'd better stay at home.

Amours

(Adult-eritis)

THE PARANOID CERTAINTY:
"I know it – she's having an affair."

THE FACILE REASSURANCE:
"I satisfy him completely."

THE OBJECTIVE TRUTH:

Yes, she is, and no, you don't.

Of men married for more than two years, 72 percent have had sex outside their marriage. Sixty-seven percent of their wives have too. After eight years of marriage the rate goes up to 84 percent of men and 79 percent of women. By 15 years it's a done deal – almost 90 percent for both sexes.

The books written by men claim that most husbands stray because married sex isn't good enough and that most women have affairs for other reasons – romance usually. Books written by women tell a different story; by their lights, women are on the prowl for the same reason as men.

There are conflicting theories about adultery, but it probably comes down to simple biology. The female Homo sapiens is in "estrus", or capable of fertilization, 12 months of the year – a rare thing in the animal kingdom – probably because we're a relatively frail race that needs all the help it can get. This means the male of the species is also able to procreate at the drop of a hat.

The big secret (which generations of male chauvinist anthropologists have tried to find some female to sweep under the rug for them) is that biologically, anthropologically, and socially, women are far more likely than men to be on the lookout for partners and far better constructed to take on all comers.

There they were, hirsute and horny Neanderthals making eyes at the ladies. The eight males were able to do the nasty three times in eight hours, with a definite drop in fertility by the second time. The three females, however, could take on all eight males as often as they were able. In order to continue the species primitive societies must have been polyandrous, one woman having more than a single mate.

But let's forget anthropology. How can you tell when your partner's having an affair?

They say they're working late at the office? A bad sign and a little out of date. Nooners are the rule these days. Almost 80 percent of affairs begin in the workplace; with more women joining the work force every day, the odds are going up. There aren't any milkmen anymore, so that's one less thing to worry about; but of the 55 percent of housewives having ongoing extramarital relationships, half are doing it with the mailman, the grocery delivery clerk or the plumber. Get suspicious if you see a lot of new copper tubing around or an overstock of canned soup.

The signs of guilt don't seem to change. Florists claim that about a third of their business still comes from men buying flowers for their girlfriends - or for their wives after having seen their girlfriends. Over-attentiveness after a drought of affection is also an indicator, as is a sudden interest in showering, especially within 30 seconds of arriving home from a "business meeting". You can also look for changes in after-shave, Marlboro butts in the ashtray, and lace panties in the laundry basket that don't belong to either of you.

Thinking about telling your mate about your dalliance? About 40 percent do, and more often than not it leads to divorce. On the other hand, 85 percent of affairs are eventually found out anyway. Console yourself with the knowledge that your partner isn't likely to get away with it, either.

HAIR
(Paranoia samsonis)

THE PARANOID CERTAINTY:
"Oh, my God, I'm losing it!"

THE FACILE REASSURANCE:
"I'm not just President of the Hair . . ."

THE OBJECTIVE TRUTH:

Hair, too much, too little or in the wrong place, is a fear shared by men and women all over the world. Baldness, specifically male pattern baldness, is the one most people - well, men - focus on.

Figuring out if you're going to go bald is easy. Go to the family photo album and take a look at your maternal grandfather - he's the one you inherit your hairiness genes from. If he was a cue ball by 50, you're likely to be one, too. One in five men starts going bald as a teenager and is very bald by 30. Another one in five keeps his full head of hair into his 60s.

If you're in your 40s and you still have a good thatch, don't congratulate yourself yet - three out of five men begin to lose hair in their late 40s and early 50s. If you're a redhead you have less to lose. The average head of mature hair has about 180,000 follicles: a redhead can have as few as 90,000. Besides, red hair is caused by a genetic defect - a lack of melanin - which leaves you wide open to skin cancer.

Women go bald too - or at least lose large clumps of hair. One in 10 shows severe hair loss by 50, and it gets worse during menopause, when one woman in three grows a mustache.

All you gorilla types who pride yourselves on the masculinity of all that fur, think again. In a recent survey in England 10 percent of women said they were actively repelled by very hairy men, 28 percent weren't attracted, 12 percent found non-hairy men more attractive than hairy, and 25 percent didn't mind hairy men as long as it wasn't in the wrong place. The back is a very wrong place - 85 percent hated back hair. A full 100 percent were thoroughly revolted by ear and nose hair.

> The average North American woman spends between $500 and $2,000 *per year* on her hair, while men spend $250 million a year on hairpieces, hair replacement, hair weaving, hair implants, and hair transplants, most of which look ridiculous.

The same group - at least, 75 percent of them - said they found bald men unattractive. Thanks a lot ladies, but you may change your tune when you hit your 40s and 50s. The cute stud muffin with the hairless chest likely has less testosterone than his hairier, balder peer. Studies have shown conclusively that men in their 40s and 50s who are bald and/or excessively hirsute have stronger sex drives, can maintain erections longer, and are capable of more sexual activity than the less hairy.

Pubic hair has become a real problem for women in the last 40 or 50 years. There are at least 25 mainstream products for removal of pubic and underarm hair. (The skinnier the bikini, the more razor burn.) Women spend more money on their hair than any other part of their health/beauty regimen. The average North American woman spends between $500 and $2,000 per year on hair. Gillette reports that women's razors, almost $400 million worth, account for a third of their revenue.

Men spend $250 million a year on hairpieces, hair replacement, hair weaving, hair implants, and hair transplants, most of which look ridiculous.

By the way, in the United States alone 650 people a year go blind due to falling eyelashes and infections caused by mascara.

GERM WARFARE

(Pasteur's Tic)

THE PARANOID CERTAINTY:
"I have all the symptoms of Anthrax."

THE FACILE REASSURANCE:
"Richard Nixon banned that stuff."

THE OBJECTIVE TRUTH:

W e're not talking the common cold here, folks, we're talking anthrax, plague, dengi-dengi, tularemia, typhoid, and yellow fever.

Sure, they banned germ warfare – (in 1925, to be exact) after seeing what the Filthy Hun's mustard gas did to the poor guys in the trenches at Ypres. Then it became the stuff of H.G. Wells novels. These days the germ warfare bogey man takes human form in the likes of Saddam Hussein, the New Age Adolf Hitler, or his second-string pal, Gaddafi. Right?

Hooey. The Brits had great barrels of the stuff at Ypres, too, but the wind just kept blowing in the wrong direction. The Allies in World War I were also working on infecting rats with plague and getting them to sneak across enemy lines. They had Sopwith Camels loaded with infected chickens, which they dropped on unsuspecting German farmers, hoping that the farmers wouldn't notice that most of them were foaming at the mouth. (The chickens, not the farmers.)

The 1925 ban, an accord signed by virtually every country in the world, was nothing more than a convenience to keep the Filthy Hun (by then known as the Beastly Boche) from starting up again.

By the mid-1930s the Americans, Canadians and Brits were putting together a hideous bouillabaisse of diseases that could be lobbed, dropped or sprayed on the enemy. Ironically the only person not actively engaged in major chemical and biological (CB) experimentation was old Adolf, who thought it tacky. Mind you, the American experimentation involved I.G. Farben, so there was probably some cross-fertilization.

The Japanese were the only ones who actually used CB warfare during WWII, but they doused the Manchurians, whom nobody seemed to care about. After the war there was high-minded talk about the fiendishness of the stuff, but they produced so much of it they had to set aside a whole atoll in the South Pacific for storage. It takes half an ounce of *bacillus anthrax* to kill a million people; the USACC has 16 tons of it on hand – for defensive purposes.

The world's largest CB warfare installation is Suffield, Alberta, a vast tract of land between Medicine Hat and Calgary. During World War II Suffield built up stocks of anthrax and developed a way of infecting German cows with rinderpest using pigeons dropped from bombers. No deadly pigeon flights are on record, but a Canadian bacteriological killer coated the bullets used to assassinate Reinhard Heydrich.

Suffield is still going strong, as are Dugway, Port Detrick, and Porton Down in England, which made a small island in the Hebrides uninhabitable for the next 500 years. The United Nations might have had some evidence that Hussein was putting together CB capability, but if they wanted to see it done right they could have looked in their own back-yard.

As you read this, more than 400 chemical and biological agents are under study in Canada, the U.S. and the U.K. – for "defensive" purposes, of course. They include anthrax, brucellosis, encephalomyelitis, black death, Rocky Mountain spotted fever, sarin and tabun (both premiered at Dachau), BZ and QQ9 (the supposed "patriotic germs", designed to kill specific racial types), cholera, ebola fever, fungu, glanders, hydrogen cyanide, Kyasanar Forest disease (the Soviet version of Agent Orange) and Marburg fever.

The U.S. government authorized the testing of delivery systems by having the entire city of New York infected by a supposedly "benign" germ through the ventilating systems of the subway, and by aerosol transmission over San Francisco. Recent spruce budworm spraying over large Canadian metropolitan areas also smacks of this kind of test run.

And remember Frank Zappa's theory that AIDS is an experiment at Fort Detrick that got out of hand? It wouldn't be the first time.

SURGERY

(St. Elsewhere Disease)

THE PARANOID CERTAINTY:
"I know he's going to leave something behind in there."

THE FACILE REASSURANCE:
"Anyone who plays golf with a two handicap must be pretty good."

THE OBJECTIVE TRUTH:

S o why do surgeons have huge amounts of malpractice insurance? The average large metropolitan hospital does about a thousand surgical procedures a day. Of those, almost a quarter are elective, which means you got talked into them. A quarter are due to specific diseases and conditions, a quarter of them relate to traumatic conditions, and the last quarter consist of outpatient surgeries such as abortions, vasectomies, and the odd accident involving poorly wielded toenail scissors.

All are potential deathtraps and many are completely unnecessary. Take hysterectomies, for instance, a hospital's top earner – a billion dollars a year in the United States alone. Of the 800,000 U.S. hysterectomies done each year almost half have no purpose but to pay office rent or put in the new swimming pool. There is also a new procedure gaining popularity among the green-masked gynecology set: the knick-knack-ectomy. The uterus is removed, along with one of the ovaries and maybe a chunk of Fallopian tube. Three months later the surgeon takes a look-see, shakes his head and tells you he's going to have to go in for the rest of the goodies. A final cash injection comes when the surgeon/gynecologist puts the now-menopausal patient on a long-term pre-scription for hormone shots and a 30-visit follow-up program. One hysterec-tomy can bring in as much as $250,000 over five years. Not bad for a 35-minute operation.

You'd think that for a payoff like that you'd get good service, even if the operation is unnecessary; but American hysterectomies are both the world's most expensive and the most likely to produce post-operative complication. Japanese surgeons can do the same operation for about $150, and they have the lowest post-operative complication rate.

Even before the surgeon picks up his scalpel you're in trouble. The average anesthetist will kill one patient and have about five close calls. A study in England tracked surgical deaths for an entire year: 300 were directly related to anesthesia and 600 more were strongly linked to it. Medical administrators will tell you that most of these deaths resulted from allergic reactions beyond the control of the surgeon or anesthetist, but it ain't so. Most occurred because of accidental, unnoticed disconnection of the anesthetic tubes; the patient died from the shock of coming to with his guts all over the table. Or because of failure to maintain an adequate airway or to provide proper ventilation. Loss of gas supply, using the wrong gas, and overdosing play their part. Some patients die because the anesthetist was out having a pee or talking to his stockbroker.

Do surgeons really leave things behind after they operate? Certainly. You have one chance in 50 of being turned into a walking trash can. Mostly it's little things - a small clamp, a non-dissolving suture or an errant piece of rubber tubing or bandage fabric - nothing serious. However, surgeons have been known to leave behind scalpels, syringes, broken saw blades, rings and surgical towels. A Boston surgeon doing a coronary bypass lost his car keys; they eventually turned up on his patient's x-ray. There is no information on whether he retrieved them or had a spare set.

A number of years ago a Canadian plastic surgeon, eventually revealed to be a raging alcoholic, misplaced 11 surgical towels during a single day's liposuctions. A Japanese surgeon once left a small transistor radio playing in his patient's abdomen, and a Harley Street surgeon accidentally dropped his wrist watch down a patient's throat while performing a routine tonsillectomy.

And let us not forget the classic, "Man Blows Up on Operating Table". You may think this is just another urban myth of the Choking Doberman sort, but there have been a number of authenticated cases of operating-room explosions caused by bowel gas. Not surprisingly, most relate to the removal of hemorrhoids, but there was one famous case involving a heart patient who had been fitted with a time-release nitroglycerin patch. When he flat-lined during surgery, electric paddles were used to try to revive him. Needless to say, the patient did not survive. We're not sure about the doctor.

FOOD ADDITIVES

("May Contain" Disease)

THE PARANOID CERTAINTY:
*"Everything on the label with an initial
is potentially lethal."*

THE FACILE REASSURANCE:
*"Everything on the label with an initial
is potentially lethal."*

THE OBJECTIVE TRUTH:

Everything on the label with an initial is potentially lethal, and shopping in a health-food store is no guarantee. Except in a very few places, the words "natural" and "organic" have no force in law – they're right up there with "new" and "improved". ("Lemon refreshed" refers to the single ounce of lemon oil put into each tank of detergent; the "spice" in the spicy spaghetti sauce is usually salt.

All those government organizations are on the lookout for our welfare, right? Sorry. Dulcin, safrole, Green #1, cobalt sulfate, cyclamates, Violet #1, Red #2, and Orange B (the coloring in Agent Orange) have all been "banned for use" by the food industry in Canada, the United States and the United Kingdom. All of them cause, variously, cancer, brain tumors, birth defects, mental retardation, radiation sickness and death. So we're safe, right? Nope. "Banned for use" doesn't mean foods containing these additives can't be imported from other countries, which they are, in huge quantities.

Among the additives not banned, and used extensively in the food industry, are Blue #1, which causes cancer (you'll find it in candy), Green #3 – bladder cancer (also found in candy), and Citrus Red #2, a variant of the banned Red #2. Those oranges from Florida that seem too good to be true? You got it, CR#2, a definite cause of seven different cancers. But don't worry, folks, they say it is "unlikely" that the coloring agent comes through the skin and into the pulp. Red #3, which makes the cherries in fruit cocktail so colorful, gives you thyroid cancer. Yellow #3, which you'll find in anything vaguely banana-ish, can cause anaphlactic shock and death in people with a reaction to Aspirin. Yellow #5, which they put in sausage meat, can give you adrenal tumors.

Relax. It gets worse.

Phosphoric acid – found in butter, baked goods, most cheese, virtually all powdered food, soda pop, breakfast cereal, processed meat and dried potatoes – has been directly linked to bone problems, including osteoporosis. Propyl gallate (in vegetable oil, potato sticks, chicken soup, and chewing gum) has shown "indications" of causing cancer.

Sodium nitrite stops nasty bacteria growing in processed foods, but is also the most potent additive carcinogen. High heat turns it into an even fouler cancer causer, and its heaviest concentrations can be found in bacon. So much for the breakfast special.

Sulphur dioxide and sodium bisulphate are added to household bleach, but they're also in dried fruit, every wine that doesn't come from France or Germany, and any processed potato product, including potato chips. Both cause severe reactions in asthmatics and anyone with respiratory problems, and destroy Vitamin B like a chemical Atilla the Hun.

Salt? High blood pressure.

Sugar? Heart disease and diabetes.

Tea? Tannic acid, potential skin cancer. Not to mention aluminum, potential Alzheimer's.

Baked beans – well, we all know about that.

You know those little sprayers fizzing dew all over the healthy-looking produce in the supermarket? A direct link has been found between them and Legionnaires' disease.

There's only one solution – stop eating.

PSYCHIATRISTS
(Freudophobia)

THE PARANOID CERTAINTY:
"They're all even crazier than I am."

THE FACILE REASSURANCE:
*"My therapist is a kind, caring human being
who is here to help me help myself."*

THE OBJECTIVE TRUTH:

The Kingdom of Shrink is guaranteed to make any sensible person pull the covers up over his head and wish he'd never been born. *Ninety percent* of psychiatrists admit to having been sexually tempted by one or more of their patients.

Ten percent of psychiatrists admit to having sexually abused one or more of their patients.

Thirty-five percent of psychiatrists admit to having been abused sexually or emotionally by one or more parents.

Fifteen percent of psychiatrists have attempted or will attempt suicide during the course of their career.

Twenty-five percent of psychiatrists admit to having had a serious drug problem at some time during their career.

Seventy-five percent of psychiatrists' marriages end in divorce (25 percent higher than the U.S. average).

Eighty-five percent of psychiatrists are in therapy themselves. (Make up your own mind about that one.)

What kind of people spend all their time listening to the morbid, nasty, sordid problems of other people? To become that kind of person, i.e., certified as a psychiatrist, requires almost 15 years of university education, which means the average psychiatrist doesn't get out of university until he or she is about 30 years old. By that time they've missed out on all those formative experiences that make the rest of us "normal".

The average shrink is not what you would call adaptable. You drag yourself into a shrink's office assuming that the doc is going to listen to your problems and treat you as an individual. Wrong. Psychiatrists, like income tax inspectors, work by the book. For the shrinks, the book is *DSM III*, a thick manual of loonie symptoms, all neatly numbered and organized. As soon as you leave the office they consult *DSM III* to see where you fit in and how you can be led back to the world of "norm". (If they can't find you in the book you're dumped into the catch-all category of 'undifferentiated borderline psychosis'.)

DSM III is cross-indexed to a cornucopia of drugs they can prescribe, ranging from phenothiazine ("care must be taken to avoid falling") to Triazolam, which can cause drowsiness, constipation, impotence, heart palpitations, seizures, blurred vision, urinary dysfunction and birth defects. Combined with alcohol, it is thought to cause violent psychotic behavior. Remember, folks, this is a drug that's supposed to stop you from feeling crazy.

If none of the drugs work your psychiatrist may prescribe electroconvulsive therapy (ECT). If you thought shock treatments went out 50 years ago, think again. Eighty percent of patients in psychiatric wards are getting them regularly. An ordinary doctor has little control over your personal life, but a psychiatrist is legally empowered to send you off to the funny farm. Once there, look out.

Except for the packaging, ECT hasn't changed over the last half-century. They give you a quick dose of insulin to send you into diabetic shock, jam a needleful of curare into your hand to keep you from flopping around too much, attach electrodes to your head, then zap you with as much current as you get from sticking each of your digits into a separate light-bulb socket.

They tell you that ECT has an 80 percent effectiveness rating. Effective for what? You lose your memory, pee your pants, and wander around looking confused until they decide to do it again. When pressed, your psychiatrist will probably admit that they think ECT makes people feel better, but they're not sure. It's one of those ideas that just stuck around.

On the other hand, if you really are crazy, you won't believe any of this anyway. Are you calling me a liar? *Are you?* ARE YOU?

DISASTER

(Cassandra's Palsy)

THE PARANOID CERTAINTY:
"If it could happen during the World Series, it could happen anytime."

THE FACILE REASSURANCE:
"The odds are in my favor."

THE OBJECTIVE TRUTH:

We're all playing bit parts in one of those movies starring Shelley Winters, Ernest Borgnine and Red Buttons - ordinary types who just happen to be on the jet that gets attacked by a terrorist missile. Or happen to be taking a trip on the ocean liner that gets hit by the tidal wave, or happen to attend a party on the top floor of the giant skyscraper with the faulty smoke alarms and the pyromaniac with oedipal problems. Those movies are so successful because, despite the fact that it's always Shelley Winters and Red Buttons, we know we're exactly the kind of poor schmucks who'll be in the wrong place at the wrong time.

And we're right.

During the San Francisco Earthquake - the Sequel, in 1989, around five million people in the Bay Area were thinking that very thing. Five million people paying no attention to the fact that the city had already been wiped out by the San Francisco Earthquake - the Mover, less than a hundred years earlier. The entire state of Florida hadn't paid attention either. Hurricane Hugo, in 1989, was a big surprise. I mean, really, folks - this is a state that builds high-rise condos on sandspits and expects Mother Nature to fake it.

There have been 395 major airline disasters in the last 30 years, most on take-off or landing, but so far no one has seen fit to use the jellied fuel, invented 25 years ago, which would save thousands of lives. They're still covering the seats with fabric that produces fatally toxic fumes when it burns.

What we need here is a cosmic Ralph Nader to put the finger on all these disasters waiting to happen. We've got crack-smoking railroad engineers towing hundreds of passengers at high speed and nuclear plants built on major fault lines (California, Nevada, Germany, Italy, France and Switzerland). We've got nuclear-waste dumps on flood plains (Washington, England, Germany, France, Japan), cities built below sea level (London, Amsterdam, Miami and Houston), and nuclear submarine bases tucked in behind the most dangerous tidal rips in the world (Cherry Point, Washington, and the Straits of Juan de Fuca). We've even got municipal engineers who dig sewers so close to major lakes that entire cities flood (downtown Chicago in 1992).

Nuclear accidents? Chernobyl is a campfire beside some of the loonie accidents. A $100 million fire and near-holocaust in Texas began when a technician, who turned out to be illiterate, went checking for a gas leak with – you guessed it – a lit candle. The first time they turned on the reactor at Chalk River, Ontario, it blew up, and a small fire at the Windscale Reactor in England has been causing cancer since 1957. Four hundred million gallons of nuclear waste have dripped into the Columbia River in Washington, and nobody ever did find that third hydrogen bomb that disappeared when the guy accidently opened the bomb-bay doors of his B-52 over the Bay of Biscay.

Cyclones in Bangladesh regularly kill tens of thousands, floods have been keeping down the population in China for centuries, and, at last count, there were 10 million rats in Mexico City, all capable of carrying bubonic plague. (There were 13 cases of bubonic plague in New York City in 1989. But that's another story.)

The number crunchers predict that, during the next five years, there is almost sure to be at least one oil spill as large if not larger than the *Exxon Valdez*, at least one major earthquake in the San Francisco area (these people just never seem to learn), and a 92 percent chance of The Big One hitting Los Angeles. You can also count on seven major airline accidents each year, seven tidal waves in the South China Sea, and a steady AIDS increase among urban heterosexual populations.

The Killer Bee scare may be over, but we still have bovine encephalitis – you know, the hamburger meat that turns your brain to Swiss cheese.

childbirth

(Spock Trauma)

THE PARANOID CERTAINTY:
"Childbirth was designed by a man."

THE FACILE REASSURANCE:
"Childbirth is a celebration of Life."

THE OBJECTIVE TRUTH:

Ah, one of Life's Little Mysteries. Women are responsible for 100 percent of births, but 91 percent of gynecologists and obstetricians are men, the same men who tell you that your gut-wrenching menstrual cramps are caused by an insistence on wage parity.

Your first clue that something is wrong is the language doctors use. Pregnancy has "symptoms", not signs; you are suffering from an illness. The "cure" involves climbing up onto a medieval torture rack, inserting your feet in stirrups, and letting a masked man shove cold metal instruments up you while another masked man croons that the enormous needle he is about to jam into the base of your spine is really for your own good, even though it may paralyze you for life.

Think about it. If God had intended women to give birth lying down on their backs babies really would be born through the navel. If that same God thought up the episiotomy, he would have given women zippers.

And what's all this about Caesarian sections? A full 25 percent of all North American childbirths are C-sections. This procedure is supposed to be used in the event of a breech presentation, in which the child is head-up rather than down. Breech presentation occurs in four of 100 births. So what about the other 21 percent?

It's all in the bottom line.

An on-call obstetrician in a hospital gets a flat rate for hanging around playing stork. The vast majority of North American births (99 percent of which take place in hospitals) are incident-free, so he has nothing to do. The C-section is the answer to both his boredom and his heavily leveraged credit cards. As soon as he picks up a scalpel and eyes your navel he's a surgeon. Surgeons get an extra fee. The same is true for the anesthetist. If he doesn't slip you an epidural or a spinal block he's on an hourly rate; but if he gives you the goodies he's on premium. Fetal monitors are also extra, as are the last-minute ultrasound and the pathologist who checks your placental afterbirth.

Then there's the department head who tells you you're primapara, so he's calling in a consulting physician and ordering half a dozen tests. Primapara? It means that this is your first child. If it's your second or 22nd they change their tactics slightly: previous births might complicate this one, so they have to call in a different specialist and order different machines.

They really get excited when you've had a C-section but want to deliver naturally this time: yours is a madness closely akin to suicide (in which case they can call in a consulting psychiatrist). In fact, a properly done C-section strengthens the uterine wall and makes natural delivery a little easier.

Your average obstetrician will tell you that an episiotomy is a surgical procedure involving the slitting of your pelvic floor from the vaginal orifice to the rectum in order to ease the pain of final delivery. He is lying. Odds are he's never imagined what it would be like to have a Swiss Army Knife open him up from fanny to testicles. Besides, the episiotomy is for his benefit, not yours. It allows him to get a better grip on the baby's head so he can pull it out faster. We're talking time and motion here: the quicker you deliver, the more babies he can do in a day and the more money he can make.

If you tell the doctor this he'll counter by telling you that during delivery almost all women tear the perineum, and he'll be telling you the truth. What he won't tell you is that a tear, with a jagged edge, will heal better than a surgical incision. It will also tighten the vaginal walls rather than loosen them, as the episiotomy does. You won't have to invest in one of those inflatable rubber doughnuts.

For everyday pregnancy paranoia, read Nancy Mitford's *The American Way of Birth* and interview as many midwives as you can find. Of course, if you didn't set the alarm on your biological clock and you're having your first kid after 40 . . .

BEING LIED TO

(Fibophobia)

THE PARANOID CERTAINTY:
"You're lying, I know it!"

THE FACILE REASSURANCE:
"I've never told a lie in my entire life."

THE OBJECTIVE TRUTH:

Liar. Of course you have. Studies show that on average we all lie at least 15 times a day. 'How are you?' 'I'm fine,' rates as a lie in most cases. Do you really want to tell the person that your marriage is crumbling, you're probably going to lose your job, and your hemmies are killing you?

For kids, Santa Claus, the Easter Bunny, and 'I Was Just Cuddling Mummy' are major lies, followed closely by 'The Dentist Is Your Friend' and 'This Isn't Going to Hurt a Bit'. From there it's only a short hop to parental guilt-inducing lies such as 'I'll Just Die if You Don't Get an A' to 'That's a Beautiful Ashtray You Made'.

Telling the cop at the breathalyzer roadblock you had only one drink probably won't work very well if the inside of your car smells like a distillery. Telling the same cop at a speed trap that your wife just went into labor is another long shot. Phoning in sick with cotton balls stuffed up your nose will work once or twice, but eventually the boss is going to get wise, as is the mom who looks at the thermometer and sees that your temperature is 112°. (Run the thermometer under lukewarm water, don't stick it up against a light bulb, kids.)

Teachers have heard every excuse in the universe for not having your homework done, and the tax people don't want to know about your leprosy. On the other hand, running an overdraft at the bank and telling the manager about your mild heart attack can work wonders.

Back in the 1950s Kinsey found that spouses lied to each other all the time, especially about money and sex. Masters and Johnson weren't surprised when the stats on sexual lies showed a marked increase by the late 1960s, and Nancy Friday is a total cynic on the subject. Women lie about orgasms all the time, and if men didn't have to get erections they'd be lying a lot more, too. Yes, Rebecca de Mornay has fantasies about Richard Gere, and yes, he has fantasies about Rebecca de Mornay, and no, neither one of them admits it.

Men lie about how much money they make, how important their jobs are, and how big their penises are. Women lie about their age, their weight, their husbands, and the number of men they've slept with. Children lie about school, friends, what happened to the cutlery, and the state of things under their beds. Governments lie about everything. Worst of all, we even lie to ourselves. Except me, of course.

The New Age

(Therapy Aversion)

THE PARANOID CERTAINTY:
"I must be 'In Denial'; everyone is in therapy except me."

THE FACILE REASSURANCE:
"My Cosmic Centeredness is in balance with my left/right brain paradigm, therefore I am One with All and in touch with the Inner Child of my Beingness."

THE OBJECTIVE TRUTH:

There is none. The whole point of the New Age is that any questioning of its non-rational tenets is an admission that you just ain't seen the light. The whirligig of New Age Woo-Wooism (NAWW) is at large on the planet. Billions of dollars are being spent each year by would-be Shirley MacLaines hell-bent for Cosmic Consciousness, and not one would admit that they're suffering from Malcolm Muggeridge Syndrome (MMS).

You probably have this dysfunction if you were brought up (a) Roman Catholic, (b) Protestant, (c) Jewish or (d) atheist – in other words, everyone might have it. MMS "survivors" usually cast off their family religious background, spent the 1960s partying, and woke up to find themselves facing Middle Age and a zero-sum afterlife. The MMS survivor is also usually (a) bored, (b) divorced or separated, and (c) not having sex. The New Age was tailor-made for these people.

Think about it. Shirley MacLaine has gotten more press from chatting to her Woo-Woo Channel/Egyptian Priestess prior self than she ever did from acting. Oprah Winfrey, Janet Jackson, and Roseanne Barr got great career mileage being "abuse" survivors. If you're not "codependent" you're "In Denial", and if you have the slightest interest in rational thought, the scientific process, or logic, your shakras are out of balance. If you're a man with an opinion on anything, you're denying your feminine self; any woman who doesn't want to run IBM is denying her right brain/male self. We have become a nation of victims, and some folks are getting rich on the fact.

Flower Essence Therapy (FET) sells you a course of lectures and potions to help you discover the right flower odor to keep you "balanced", even if you weren't listing noticeably. It would appear that FET is a variant of AromaTherapy (AT), which involves your "personal" smell. The potential for improvisational comedy is obvious, but suffice it to say that a practitioner in Boulder, Colorado, goes by the name of Breath Wildheart. Uh-huh.

If you're a guy, how about "Male Empowerment" à la Robert Bly. *Iron John* had men going out into the woods and beating drums from one end of the continent to the other. Bly's speciality involves "wounds to our Princehood", "Zeus Energy" and "the genuine patriarchy that brings down the sun through the Sacred King." Hey, real men don't lie.

There are as many therapies as there are "codependent", "dysfuntional", "in denial" people on the planet. There's "Electric Tanka" – two nine-volt batteries and a mantra – "Beyond 20/20", which says they can cure cataracts through herbal essences; Colon Therapy (sensible Brits call this bum-fetishism), which involves six quarts of soapy water squirted up you on the way to nirvana; "Somatic Experiencing Hypnotherapy", which roughly translates as sleeping on the therapist's couch for half an hour; "Soul Retrieval Therapy", in case you lost yours somewhere; Lomi-Lomi, Huna and Hakomi, "Ancient Hawaiian Healing Arts", and one that defies explanation, Transpersonal Empowerment Emergence (TEE).

Who are these people? They'll all tell you they are "certified" but who's doing the certifying? There are 2,200 sex therapists in North America, but no licensing body. A Certified Colon Therapist (CCT) has gone to some place like the NCTI, the National Colon Therapy Institute, for a seminar at which hundreds of people run around trying to stick rubber tubes up one another. A certificate from the Counsellor Training Institute (CTI) allows you to certify other therapists.

I find all this a bit hard to take, but then, I am Unrepentantly In Denial (UID).

F O O D

(Noshophobia maximus)

THE PARANOID CERTAINTY:
"Everything causes cancer."

THE FACILE REASSURANCE:
"A balanced diet is the best life insurance."

THE OBJECTIVE TRUTH:

According to the normally happy-go-lucky people at the World Health Organization the only unpolluted water table left in the world is located slightly east of Ulan Bator and is incapable of growing anything except dust storms.

Not everything causes cancer, but it's close. So if you want to spend twice as much for "organic" bananas, be my guest; but you won't do yourself any good, especially if you're under six years of age. Let me walk you through the problem.

Under "A" we have alfalfa sprouts, almonds, amaranth flour, anchovies and apples. Alfalfa sprouts are high in residual peremethrin, a carcinogen. Traces of the pesticide were found in 20 percent of American domestic sprouts, and 22 percent of the imported ones.

Almond butter is even more toxic than almonds, which spoil quickly, increasing the toxicity of the parathion pesticide they are sprayed with.

Anchovies suck up whatever pollution is in the waters they swim in, including PCB, DDT, dieldrin and heptachloride – all carcinogenic.

Apples are anathema. The most common apple pesticide is Carbyral, which causes damage to the liver, kidneys and central nervous system, not to mention testicular atrophy if you eat a lot of them. Apple juice, apple sauce and apple cider are often treated with Alar, a compound that concentrates the toxins already present in the apples.

You should also know that the wormiest, maggot-ridden apples are the ones used in apple sauce, juice and baby food. The wax on the nice rosy red ones is severely toxic.

Bananas are all sprayed with Aldercarb, a variant of the nerve gas used at Dachau and Auschwitz manufactured by the Rhone Poulenc Company of France. As well, most bananas are shipped green and force-ripened by exposure to cyanide, a residue of which is left on the skins. Aldercarb was found in 17 percent of all bananas shipped into the United States in 1992; cyanide was present in 100 percent of the samples tested.

The "B"s are also a minefield of snacking dangers. Bacon is full of carcinogenic dieldrin and nitrites. (If the toxins don't get you the cholesterol and fats will.)

Barley is full of endosulfans, which cause kidney trouble and shrivelled testicles. Barracudas cause brain damage, and fresh-water bass is loaded with mercury, especially if you happened to catch it in the Great Lakes.

Beef, of course, is as bad as bacon. Federal inspectors both in the United States and in the United Kingdom check only for visible problems – they couldn't care less about the resident DDT, PCB, aflatoxins, and tumor-causing and sex-altering female hormones. Beer has all the evils found in barley, and beets are drowned in malathion, which can cause severe central nervous system problems.

The "B"s continue with bluefish and bonito, both containing mercury, PCB, DDT, and dieldrin. Bologna has everything you find in beef (and a lot more), and the unspeakably foul lindane.

Fifty-one percent of all boysenberries tested showed toxic levels of nine different organophosphate pesticides, including an Agent Orange derivative. Brazil nuts are loaded with pesticides the U.S. government banned years ago, and happen to be the most naturally radioactive food in the world.

George Bush – also a "B" – appears to have been right not to like broccoli. A memo quietly circulated by the American FDA and the food and drug authorities in Great Britain indicates that broccoli contains one of the highest levels of pesticide residues. Cooking reduces some of the toxins, but most pesticides remain deep within the vegetable.

"C" foods you should avoid include carrots – diazanium and dieldrin, endosulfans, and linuron. Carp are full of PCBs. So are catfish, which are also chock full of mercury. So much for Cajun cooking.

Carrot juice is full of benomyl, a hard-hitting mutagen that can cause sexual development problems in pregnancy. Casaba melons can cause chronic liver damage. Cashews, in addition to causing liver damage, produce a natural toxin similar to the one in poison ivy. If you're allergic to poison ivy and eat a few "organic" cashews be ready for anaphlactic shock, heart failure, and paralysis, not to mention death.

Celery is a death trap, especially the imported stuff. As well as containing a whole shelf-full of pesticides, slightly wilting celery begins to produce a natural toxin called psoralens, which causes skin irritations.

Cherries are the worst "C" of all, with more than 11 pesticide residues, including captan. Not only is captan a carcinogen, but its structure is almost identical to thalidomide.

I'm going to stop at "C", but nary a veggie or meat product seems to be safe to eat, right down to the dastardly zucchini, waxed with cancer-causing compounds and chock full of parathion, chlordane, toxaphene, dieldrin, heptachlor and seven fungicides.

Bon appetit, folks.

BEING SCREWED

(Phillips Head Phobia)

THE PARANOID CERTAINTY:
"They're all out to get me."

THE FACILE REASSURANCE:
"If you treat them fairly, they'll treat you fairly."

THE OBJECTIVE TRUTH:

The concept of "Being Screwed" is like having a "non-specific sexually transmitted disease"; no one knows exactly what it is, but you sure as hell know you've got it. There are endless ways of being screwed, from the guy who short-changes you at the parking lot to the loftiest heights of government.

Any accountant will tell you that the average computerized bank statement has about two mistakes a month. Oddly, those mistakes are almost never in your favor. The banks don't tell you about the enormous "clearing house" account they operate. Take a check into a bank and they'll tell you it's going to take five business days to clear. In fact, the check is debited within minutes of being deposited, and credited to the bank's 'clearing house' account. There it sits for the next five days, gathering interest like moss on a stone that's stopped rolling. Add your check to the tens of thousands of other checks waiting to be "cleared" and you have a hefty chunk of change. Literary and entertainment agents play the same game, taking in money for their clients, holding on to it 30 to 60 days, and pocketing the resulting interest. Both banks and accountants average out amounts, shaving a penny here and a penny there, shifting them into their own accounts. This is also a favorite game of large corporations and public utilities. Watch out for the phrase "amounts rounded off"; it's a dead giveaway.

The income tax people are Master Screwsmen. Every month your paycheck is nicked for an amount based on your overall salary. Your employer passes on the loot; the income tax folks hold on to it until tax time. You submit your return and ask for a refund. Eventually it reaches you, but until then the government has had your money basically interest-free.

Lawyers are useful when you want to fight back against being screwed, but they have their own tricks. One lawyer told me that virtually all his colleagues overbill each hour of service by as much as 25 percent. How many of us have received bills from lawyers and simply taken them at face value? Check up on your lawyer through "Fee Taxing". As a client you have a perfect right to contact the Bar Association and have your lawyer's fees "taxed", i.e., audited. The Bar Association is legally bound to investigate and judge whether the fees have been boosted out of line with the work done. In the United States, seven out of 10 requests for fee taxing result in a return of funds to the client. In the U.K. the ratio is six out of 10.

One of the best scams involves roofing. The roofer goes up on top of your house with a Polaroid camera and comes back with a glossy snap that may have been taken on the moon. While you stare at the pits and yawning chasms in "your" roof, he's hitting his calculator. The pictures may not be your roof at all, but it's not likely that you'll go up to check.

Home shopping clubs screw you by video, chuckling all the way to the bank while you get dozens of UPS deliveries. Just what kind of idiot were you to pick up the phone and buy that "porcelain" set of the Seven Dwarfs?

The tendency, of course, is to screw back in direct proportion to being screwed. This might account for a recent figure that shows a 20 percent "underground economy" in North America - $70 billion to $90 billion a year is moved throughout the system invisibly and untaxed. One U.S. economist predicts that by the year 2000 almost half of the American Gross National Product will be under the table. The underground in New Zealand has virtually bankrupted the country, and in Canada it costs twice as much to collect GST as it produces in revenue. Of course, if you're being an honest citizen and not taking part in the re-screwing, you get screwed again, carrying the added burden placed on the economy by the screwers.

SEXUALLY TRANSMITTED...
(Immaculata's Conundrum)

THE PARANOID CERTAINTY:
"I'm going to have to cover my entire body with Saran Wrap."

THE FACILE REASSURANCE:
"Pennicillin cured all that. And anyway, I use condoms and practise safe sex."

THE OBJECTIVE TRUTH:

There's no such thing. As this one goes the Vatican's right on the money: sex is dangerous and that's that. A hundred years ago they used to boil your privates in oil to cure syphilis and feed you lead salts to cure gonorrhea, but in these strange times STDs have gotten completely out of hand, in spite of the wonders of modern medicine.

Sixteen million new cases of gonorrhea are reported each year worldwide; 750,000 are American teenagers and 3 million each year are British. There are a mere 7 million cases of syphilis a year, but the real comer is chlamydia, with 5 million new cases each year and no sign of slowing down. On top of that we've got herpes, hepatitis B, AIDS, genital warts, trichomoniasis, scabies and crabs. There's a myth that sex is on the wane, but 75 million new cases of sexually transmitted diseases a year tell us that a lot of people out there are still doing it.

Regardless of what the Julius M. Schmidt company and the surgeon general of the United States say, condoms aren't stemming the tide. It's not surprising. Most sexually transmitted diseases can be caught by a dozen varieties of physical contact. It may not be politically correct to say so, but you can get trich and chlamydia from towels, clothing, kissing, chlorinated water and hot tubs. And, yes, maybe even from the toilet seat, but only if you remain in contact with it for at least 45 minutes. (Unless you're constipated or read *The New York Times* in the biffy you're probably safe.)

You can catch herpes from all sorts of sexual play, and there still isn't a cure. Pubic lice (crabs) and scabies can also be contracted through clothing and non-intercourse sexual contact.

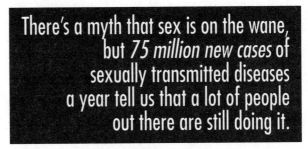

There's a myth that sex is on the wane, but *75 million new cases* of sexually transmitted diseases a year tell us that a lot of people out there are still doing it.

Both men and women can catch yeast infections, the most prevalent form of sexually transmitted disease. The most common yeast infection is monillia, with a relative newcomer, gardnerella, coming in a close second. These infections tend to ping-pong back and forth between partners. The difficulty is made worse because the topical "cures" inevitably rob a woman's mucous membranes of the very antibodies that keep yeast infections at bay. As well, the chemicals used in tampons and feminine napkins also promote the growth of the fungus.

If you like worrying about this kind of thing check out STD exotics such as Moroccan blue balls, ureaplasma, *hemophilius ducreyei, lymphogranulum venereum* and *granuloma inguinale*.

Me, I'm off to buy that extra-strength Saran Wrap and a dictionary.

DISEASES

GOING TO T

(Welby's Colic or Kildarephobia)

THE PARANOID CERTAINTY:
"He's going to tell me I'm dying."

THE FACILE REASSURANCE:
"I've never been sick a day in my life."

THE OBJECTIVE TRUTH:

During the next 12 months we will make 3.7 million visits to the doctor throughout the Western world. A lot of us are going to wish we'd stayed home. Four percent will be told that we have high blood pressure and 50 percent of those diagnosed with the problem will be dead within two years.

Three and a half percent of women going to the doctor for a routine check-up will discover that they're pregnant; of those, only 46 percent will be pleased at the rabbit's passing. Another 3 percent will find that they have an unspecified infection, and be referred to a specialist; 2.7 percent

HE DOCTOR

will be diagnosed as having a severe respiratory problem such as emphysema or lung cancer; 2.2 percent will suddenly discover that we have diabetes; 1.6 percent will be diagnosed as having pharyngitis, and 1 percent will go directly from the doctor's office to the VD clinic; 1.4 percent will discover that we're crazy, and 0.9 percent will be diagnosed as having a severe heart problem requiring open-heart surgery. One percent each will have cataracts, glaucoma, and asthma, and 0.9 percent will be deemed arthritic. Stay at home and send an apple instead.

In the United States 74,000 people will be diagnosed as having AIDS; 54,000 people previously diagnosed as having the disease will die – 65 percent will be homosexual; 19 percent will be drug users; 7 percent will be gay drug users; and 1 percent will be hemophiliacs. Of the women who contract AIDS 50 percent will be drug users, 35 percent will get it from heterosexual contact; and 7 percent will get it from blood transfusions during elective surgery. The overall rate of heterosexual AIDS will increase by 22 percent per year.

Have a nice day.

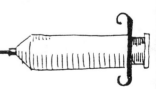

#

(Never-Ending Story Disease)

THE PARANOID CERTAINTY:
*"My mother-in-law is going to drop in for a three-week
visit 24 hours before a tax audit."*

THE FACILE REASSURANCE:
"Mi casa est su casa."

THE OBJECTIVE TRUTH:

Not only is your mother-in-law going to drop in 24 hours before a tax audit, she's going to wait for the tax audit to happen. She's doing it on purpose. A mother-in-law hates you, by definition. You stole away her child, you are having sex with her child, and there is no way you can take care of her child as well as she can. She has an insatiable need to see what's in your underwear drawer, medicine cabinet and bank accounts. She is also going to lecture you on child-rearing, cooking and laundry.

All house guests are mothers-in-law in disguise. If you live in a large North American or European city or in what most people deem to be vacation spots, suddenly, courtesy of regularly scheduled or charter flights, "Old Bob", the nerd you hated in high school, is going to drop in, trailing a line of Samsonites. If you're very lucky "Old Bob" will call you from the airport asking for directions to your house. If he does, lie.

Once resident, Guests rarely leave. They also have some food problem that necessitates you cook nothing containing wheat, dairy, or food additives. They may be vegetarians, and are likely to belong to a fringe religion or group. They will put dents in your car, steal your cutlery and take out loans in your name. They will break things and not replace them. They will not do laundry or help with the cooking. They will tell you all their problems, try to borrow money and develop serious diseases while in your care. They will use your telephone to place lengthy calls to area codes you didn't know existed.

You will not have sex while they are in your house because Guests inevitably stay up later than you do, watching television directly below or beside your bedroom. You will fight with your spouse, continually and in whispers. Once allowed to enter your premises, they will destroy you.

Don't be fooled by "a day or two", or "just until we get settled". Lies, all lies. If the food is good, the weather sunny, and there's a beach nearby they'll stay all summer. If you live close to a ski hill they'll help decorate the Christmas tree, borrow your boots and put their picture on your tow pass.

Beware especially of the people who describe themselves as "The Perfect House Guests". These are the ones who never so much as scrape a plate, but deign to brighten your life with a box of stale, hard-center chocolates when and if they ever leave.

The only effective defense against House Guests is sloth. Make yourself, your children, your spouse, your automobile and your home unfit for human habitation at the first sign of invasion. Do not take out the garbage, hide most of the cutlery, and make sure the refrigerator is virtually empty. Reload the lint trap in the dryer. As a last resort, after the kids are in bed, suggest a nude, midnight barbecue, followed by group sex in the living room, accompanied by a continuous slide show of vacation snaps. Murmur about the sensuous secrets of microwaved marshmallows applied to strategic parts of the body.

Then offer to call them a taxi.

DEATH

(Reaper's Creep)

THE PARANOID CERTAINTY:
"The doctor said it was only indigestion but . . ."

THE FACILE REASSURANCE:
"I eat margarine so I'm okay."

THE OBJECTIVE TRUTH:

With the exception of a few shrewd people like Walt Disney, this is one paranoia that even George Burns can't ignore. The average life expectancy for North American men is around 71 years; for women it's 78 years and two months. In other words, if you were born in 1912 or earlier, chances are you're not reading this.

The oldest people in the world supposedly live in the Caucasus mountains of Georgia. They drink like fish and smoke like chimneys, and one of them lived to be 167 years old. The average age seems to be around 106. Most authorities put this longevity down to altitude, trace elements in the vodka, and something in the yogurt they eat. I think it's simply a result of

lying. When you're 167 years old, who's around to contradict you? (In England they've researched tombstones claiming that people lived to incredible ages and discovered that the stonemasons just couldn't add straight.)

On the off chance that Georgians really do live to those ripe old ages you could go out and buy yourself wholesale lots of vodka and yogurt, but you'd probably be wasting your time. Most vodka is full of fusil oil, which is poisonous, and yogurt has absolutely no healthy effect if it's pasteurized or if sugar has been added. In Poland they simply set saucers of milk out to rot and then eat it, but this just encourages various other bugs.

Wine is also supposed to be good for long life, but I don't see it doing the heavy-drinking people of France much good. They have the highest European incidence of sclerosis of the liver, and two out of three French automobile accidents are alcohol-related.

Some say that vegetarians live longer, but there doesn't seem to be much real evidence to back this up. The Veggie Storm Troopers who loudly proclaim the horrors of red meat inevitably forget that one of the most famous vegetarians was Adolf Hitler. Historically, vegetarian societies have usually been extremely poor and most fell to meat-eating conquerors. Did Genghis Khan ever order a small salad with lemon-juice dressing, no bacon bits?

94

Geography does seem to have a lot to do with life span. Temperate climates like North America's and Europe's produce greater life expectancies than those of tropical countries. But lifestyle is a big factor too – the more stress, and the larger the community you live in, the shorter the life span. People in Los Angeles, New York and London have shorter average life spans than their rural counterparts.

The major insurance companies have long known that people who smoke and drink have virtually the same life expectancy as their less sinning counterparts, but if your mother smoked or drank immediately prior to or during her pregnancy your life expectancy can drop by as much as 20 percent. We all know that our chances of lung disease increase in direct proportion to both the amount we smoke and the tar and nicotine count. But we tend to forget that the lighter the cigarette smoked, the greater the risk. People who choose light cigarettes aren't fooling the little addiction button in their heads: smoke lighter, suck harder is the norm. This causes the smoke to be drawn deeper into the lungs and held there for a longer period.

Of the hundreds of weird "cures" for aging Placenta Therapy and Parabiosis are particularly paranoia-inducing. Placenta Therapy involves regularly snacking on human placenta (origin unknown), which supposedly drops your blood-sugar level and cholesterol count while increasing sexual function. The main proponent of this ritual (other than a few anthropology professors) is Alekpher Mehtiev of Odessa. Unfortunately, Dr. M. hasn't been heard of since the rise of Boris Yeltsin. Parabiosis is right out of an old Peter Cushing movie. The blood of young people (maximum age: 19) is transfused into older patients. Unless you're willing to travel to São Paulo, Brazil and get friendly with a bunch of hot-blooded tribesmen who'll top you up for ten grand a session, forget it. The doctor in charge of the biggest clinic down there is Walther Sawitsch, who got the idea during World War II in Lithuania. What *were* you doing in '42, Walther?

Creating a Personal Paranoia
for the 1990s...

Paranoia is no longer the private fiefdom of the lunatic fringe. Indeed, people without their own paranoia for the nineties are apt to be social misfits.

Dorothy Parker was so afraid of dying without a meaningful epithet on her lips that she spent a great deal of time coming up with an endless variety of bons mots. Richard Nixon had a thing about telling the truth, George Bush is frightened of broccoli, and Imelda Marcos wouldn't be caught dead without the right pair of shoes – probably a variation on the classic fear of being in a traffic accident wearing two-day-old underwear.

Not having a personal paranoia has become a paranoia in itself: neuroparanoiavacans – the fear of being boringly well-adjusted. This is most commonly found among the rich and famous, many of whom worry about being too normal for their station in life. What would Jack Nicholson be without his anti-social snarl, and would you hire Marlon Brando if his fat, mumblings, and lip-biting were mere gluttony, bad diction, and lack of Chapstick?

There is no longer a place for the Fred MacMurrays and James Stewarts of the world, something Jimmy Carter discovered too late in his career. To be without a paranoia is to be nothing.

The answer, of course, is to create a paranoia all your own, but you have to follow the rules.

Political correctness: any fear associated with animals is out. Rats, bats and beetles all have their place in the ecological chain. You might be able to get away with a fear of cockroaches, but it's unimaginative and dies at dinner parties.

A morbid fear of aerosols will get you some points – you can reel back in horror when you spot somebody using oven cleaner; go ahead – blink rapidly and hyperventilate at the first whiff of hair spray.

Refrigerators are a good paranoia focus. They have a nice, subtle appeal, as it's not the fridge so much as the ecological terror of the freon used in the cooling system.

It is best to avoid the common-or-garden variety of paranoia. Agora-phobia (fear of open spaces) might cramp your style in work and social situations. You might, however, specialize in a fear of rock concerts or sporting events in domed stadiums located in earthquake-prone zones.

Claustrophobia, too, is a bit old hat; instead, refine it to a fear of being buried alive. Taphophobia, or fear of premature burial, has some solid cultural history (for instance, Poe's "Tomb of Ligeia") as well as some modern-day sociological implications (exotic compounds used by voodoo priests).

At all costs avoid taking on a paranoia which you can't pronounce. Fear of having 13 people at the dinner table is wonderfully exotic, but just try saying triskaidekophobia after more than one glass of California Cabernet. The same is true for didaskaleinophobia (fear of school) and achluophobia (fear of the dark).

In the final analysis it's probably best to avoid most of the really exotic paranoias such as fear of the passage of specific periods of time (chronophobia) or infinity (apierophobia). You'll rarely have the opportunity to put them to use unless you're in involuntary therapy and you want to give the shrink a lift (or if you write for a living – in which case anything goes because everyone expects writers to be crazy).

Instead, concoct a paranoia of your own. Homodermoiophobia is a possibility. Dermophobia is a fear of skin, iophobia is a fear of rust, and homo is a nice overall catchword that means anything vaguely human. Put them together and you have a fear of birth-marks. It's neat and has a nice ring to it, and you can talk about it endlessly.

Try making your paranoia a useful one. If you have zippophobia no one is going to mind when you repeat your address several times to make sure they've got it right. Or a few dark words about your tragic case of RR syndrome (Ronalds-Reynolds phobia) will keep smokers at bay.

The intelligent paranoiac in the 1990s will keep a few unspoken paranoias to hand in case of emergencies – when your suburban neighbor suggests taking the kids to McDonald's for the upcoming birthday party your overwhelming bozophobia (fear of clowns) combined with a dose of junk food phobia should do the trick nicely. Bell's phobia, sometimes known as Sprint's terror, can also be handy on those long-distance calls that go beyond your budget.

Make sure you know as much about your phobia as possible. My own long-standing paranoia of choice is an old-fashioned fear of flying, first discovered in mid-Atlantic in a DC-8 stretch. Halfway to Europe one of the port-side engines blew up, taking 20 feet of wing with it. All 186 passengers aboard (myself included) vomited simultaneously as we plummeted towards the waves below. I haven't been the same since, but I do know as much about flying as most Federal Aviation Authority crash investigators. Name me an aircraft and I can quote you its glide ratio and wing-load statistics.

This is of fundamental importance if you expect people to believe in your fear and give you the sympathy you so richly deserve. No one is going to feel for your alopecia nervosa if you have a full head of hair, but being able to give pertinent statistics about divorce will lend credence to your gamophobia. If you have an aversion to the New Agers insisting that they were one of Jack the Ripper's victims in a previous life you'd better know why the northern angle of the Great Pyramid explains that rash of airplane disappearances over the Bermuda Triangle; for, of all modern fears, fringeophobia or millenniumitis requires the most ongoing research.

For professional paranoiacs like myself, and for the serious paranoia hobbyist, life presents an infinite variety of fears (panophobia – the fear of everything), and you'll probably wind up carrying around a combination. As well as being aerophobic (afraid to fly) I also suffer from otisophobia (fear of elevators), mild arachnophobia (fear of spiders) and a serious case of auditophobia maximus (fear of the tax man). At times an overload of paranoias can have its drawbacks (I haven't flown since 1976) but my fear of elevators, preventing me from attending meetings in tall buildings, has led to a large number of free meals in nearby hotel restaurants.

This, of course, is the true value of a well-honed paranoia – you are making fear work for you. When someone panders to your paranoia he is, by definition, deferring to you. Some people, like Stephen King, have made millions out of this very basic form of manipulation. Virtually all of King's novels are paranoia-based and he'll happily admit that most of the things he writes about are those he's afraid of himself.

If you do decide that paranoia is for you, by all means enjoy yourself. It's a frightening world out there. If you can't make the best of it back up your pessimism with at least one comforting fear you can call your own.

One more thing – if you have your own personal paranoia and a story to tell about it, I'd love to hear from you. *The Paranoid's Handbook* is only the tip of the iceberg and since I'm not even slightly zenophobic (afraid of strangers), feel free to tell me your strangest, funniest and most deeply rooted terrors.

Even if you're confidophobic (afraid of telling secrets) I can promise you absolute anonymity. Of course, when all is said and done, the true paranoid will assume that everything I've said has been a lie. This is a classic paranoia in its own right – skeptophobia or *The New York Times* disease, the fear of believing the printed word. Frightening, isn't it?

A Paranoid's Glossary
of Fearful Things

The following is a brief glossary of potential sources of paranoia found in the day-to-day world. It is by no means complete and care should be taken against concluding that your lack of fear of the items mentioned is a *de facto* clean bill of health.

Aerosols
Anything you can spray out of a can from hair spray to fake whipped cream. In some countries it contains freon, a propellant gas that can cause heart attacks, lung cancer, headaches, nausea, dizziness, shortness of breath, burns, lung inflammation and brain damage. In extreme cases it may also cause coma and death.

Asbestos
Autopsy reports in the United States, the United Kingdom and Europe have shown that 100 percent of people who live in urban locations have some damage caused by asbestos. Asbestos exposure affects every organ in the body. Diseases caused by long-term exposure to this substance include asbestosis and mesothelioma, a fatal form of cancer. There is no safe level of exposure.

Aspartame
An artificial sweetener that can cause widespread brain damage among children and rapid behavior change in people prone to Alzheimer's disease and Parkinson's.

Benzene
The stuff you find in most bottled waters in the health food store. Causes brain and liver damage. Allergic responses include drunkenness, lightheadedness, disorientation, loss of appetite and fatigue. Linked to Yuppie Flu or chronic fatigue syndrome.

Dirt
Particularly dangerous if you are visiting Aunt Em down on the farm. Even a small scratch exposed to pig manure can cause gas gangrene, which differs from ordinary gangrene in its swiftness of growth. Gas gangrene can cause suppuration on an entire limb within 15 to 20 minutes. Death can be prevented only by radical and immediate amputation of the infected limb.

Disposable Lighters
Not only are they made from environmentally unfriendly plastics and loaded with even more unfriendly butane gas, but studies have also shown that disposable lighters have a failure rate of over 6 percent. This has led to a number of lawsuits for serious burn injuries caused by explosions in pockets and purses.

Doors
Fifteen percent of all household accidents in the United Kingdom involve impact with a door. Twelve percent of serious-injury accidents in the United States involve doors. The most common form of door accident involves being struck by a door being opened from the other side.

Elevators
Between 20 and 25 percent of elevators in the United States are uninspected for at least a year. Elevator statistics for fatal accidents per mile travelled are 50 times greater that those for passenger miles travelled in commercial aircraft.

Eyeglasses
Twenty-five percent of all blinding eye injuries are caused by people poking themselves in the eye with their own glasses. Spectacles have also been used as a murder weapon.

Fires
Most fatal fires come about as a result of smoking in bed. The cigarettes are bad enough, but the bed manufacturers make it worse by failing to use non-flammable materials. Almost all electric blankets, the second-largest cause of fatal fires, contain toxic fume-producing fabric.

Fluoride
You brush your teeth with it, and most urban water supplies are liberally laced with it to cut down on *e. coli* bacteria. Fluoride is a known carcinogen. It is also used to poison rats.

Fragrance
The manufacturers of that lovely-smelling stuff you put onto your throat and behind your ears never list their ingredients, most of which are artificial and many of which can cause headaches, dizziness, rashes, skin discoloration, violent coughing and vomiting. My Sin, indeed.

Friends
They come in many varieties, the most common of which are the Fair Weather and the In Need.

Hydrogenated Oil
You find it in your coffee creamer and cheap milk shakes. It causes cancer and contributes to neurological disease, hardening of the arteries, skin diseases and cataracts.

Lawyers
Fifty percent of the lawyers in the United States admit that they overcharge their clients on a regular basis. Thirty percent of lawyers admit that they do not enjoy their jobs. The good news is that lawyers have a life span roughly 10 years less than the norm.

Lead

Check the paint in that house you just bought. Lead causes pain, loss of appetite, constipation, growth problems in children, miscarriage, cramps, excessive thirst and nausea. If you have a small child, look out. Lead-based paint is a known contributor to sudden infant death syndrome and Reye's syndrome, which is usually fatal.

Mineral Oil

A carcinogen as well as being utterly useless as a sexual lubricant. Banned as a food additive in Germany.

Mothers-in-Law

According to the U.S. Psychiatric Association 35 percent of all marriage failures list the mother-in-law as a contributing factor to the breakdown.

Pesticides

Effects of pesticides include paralysis, neuritis, sterility, convulsions, dizziness, weakness, enlarged pupils, blurred vision, muscle twitching, slowed heartbeat, aplastic anemia, nausea, cough, vomiting, diarrhea, tremors, liver damage, kidney damage and brain damage. They also alter menstrual periods and decrease sexual function.

Plastics

Plexiglass causes cancer; so does epoxy. Bakelite releases formaldehyde when it burns. Polyester causes skin irritation, and polyvinyl chloride causes Raynaud's disease.

Wrist-watches

One out of five people who wear those outsize diver's watches eventually develop tendonitis. On the other hand, the Seiko diver's watch is standard issue to CIA field agents and is a highly effective form of brass knuckles.

Why is this page blank?...